# Unlocking Formative Assessment

# Unlocking Formative Assessment

## Practical strategies for enhancing pupils' learning in the primary classroom

# Shirley Clarke

Assessment, Guidance and Effective Learning (AGEL),
Institute of Education, University of London

Hodder & Stoughton

A MEMBER OF THE HODDER HEADLINE GROUP

Orders: please contact Bookpoint Ltd, 130 Milton Park, Abingdon, Oxon OX14
4SB. Telephone: (44) 01235 827720, Fax: (44) 01235 400454. Lines are open from
9.00 – 6.00, Monday to Saturday, with a 24 hour message answering service.
Email address: orders@bookpoint.co.uk

*British Library Cataloguing in Publication Data*
A catalogue record for this title is available from The British Library

ISBN 0 340 80126 3

First published 2001
Impression number    10 9 8 7 6 5 4 3 2 1
Year        2005 2004 2003 2002 2001

Cover photo: Sally and Richard Greenhill
Typeset by Dorchester Typesetting Group Limited
Printed in Great Britain for Hodder & Stoughton Educational,
a division of Hodder Headline Plc, 338 Euston Road, London NW1 3BH
by J. W. Arrowsmith Ltd., Bristol

# Contents

## Acknowledgements

I would like to thank the following schools and local education authorities (LEAs) for allowing me to use examples of their teachers' or their children's work. It is their examples of formative assessment in action that bring the book to life and help teachers see what is possible:

Bounds Green Junior School, Haringey
Conway Infant School, Greenwich
Deansfield Primary School, Greenwich
Drew Primary School, Newham
Dunmow Junior School, Essex
Lingfield Primary School, Surrey
Loddon Junior School, Earley
Nanpean Primary School, Cornwall
Prettygate Infant School, Essex
Priory Lower School, Bedfordshire
Ridgeway Primary School, Croydon
St Ives Infant School, Cornwall

St John the Baptist Primary School, Tower Hamlets
Sir John Cass Primary School, City of London
Whitehawk Primary School, Brighton
William Cobbett Junior School, Surrey

Cornwall LEA
Essex LEA
Manchester LEA
Norwich LEA
Nottinghamshire LEA

I would also like to thank the following people:

- My husband, Barry Silsby, for his support and love and for being the head of an exemplary primary school!

- My editor, Chas Knight, for his incredible attention to detail and his wisdom about education, despite never having trained as a teacher.

- All the teachers who have attended my short courses on assessment at the Institute of Education. It is from them that I am continually learning how to convert theory into practice.

- The teachers involved in the exciting Cornwall Formative Assessment Project.

- All the teachers, across the country, who have given me such enthusiastic feedback about my work, keeping me focused on what really matters.

**Shirley Clarke**

Please e-mail me on sclarke@shirleyclark.demon.co.uk if you have any feedback about the strategies outlined in this book, which would be useful to other teachers. This is action research!

# Introduction

## The purpose of this book

*Unlocking Formative Assessment* is the follow-up to *Targeting Assessment in the Primary Classroom* (Clarke, 1998), which broke new ground in describing, in practical terms, how formative assessment strategies might look in the classroom. The success of that book was largely due to the source of its ideas – the tried and tested methods of hundreds of teachers and schools shared at INSET courses with me at the Institute of Education or in my research projects. Over the last three years, my work with teachers has been continuing, on an even larger scale, and there is now so much more to add.

*Unlocking Formative Assessment* takes the strategies further and deeper, shows more examples of teachers' systems, and introduces three new aspects of formative assessment: monitoring, questioning and self-esteem. It also provides more links with established research. The section on marking is particularly well developed, as a result of my own research interests in this area.

## The current context

**Formative assessment** has at last become a term known to most educators in the UK. Over a period of ten years, understandings of assessment have developed from a notion of ongoing assessment as no more than regular summative assessments, through a middle period of more child-centred approaches via records of achievement, portfolios or significant achievement folders, to a more comprehensive picture of what really makes children progress.

Although much has been said about the differences between summative and formative assessment, I believe we need to simplify this argument in order to get on with developing classroom strategies which help children to learn. My definition of the two types of assessment, through a gardening analogy, hopefully adds to the continuing understanding of purposes of assessment:

*If we think of our children as plants...* **summative** *assessment of the plants is the process of simply measuring them. The measurements might be interesting to compare and analyse, but, in themselves, they do not affect the growth of the plants.* **Formative** *assessment, on the other hand, is the garden equivalent of feeding and watering the plants – directly affecting their growth.*

Formative assessment describes *processes of teaching and learning,* whereas summative assessment takes place *after* the teaching and learning.

# The turning point:
# Black and Wiliam's findings

By 1997, the assessment emphasis from Government in England was quite clearly focused on **summative** assessment. Even Teacher Assessment was described as the end-of-key-stage levelling process, rather than the ongoing understanding of children's understanding. A group of assessment academics, naming themselves the Assessment Reform Group, decided that something significant needed to happen to convince policymakers to change their emphasis, or even just to acknowledge the power of **formative** rather than summative assessment.

To that end, Paul Black and Dylan Wiliam, from King's College, University of London, were commissioned to find out whether or not formative assessment could be shown to raise levels of attainment. The pair embarked on a year's work, trawling through all the studies since 1988 which involved aspects such as sharing learning goals, pupil self-evaluation and feedback. Many studies were rejected through lack of rigour, as Black and Wiliam decided to take account only of those where a control group had been set up and children had been tested before and after the trial, so that learning gains could be measured and compared.

They found that formative assessment strategies do indeed raise standards of attainment, with a greater effect for children of lower ability. At GCSE they were able to calculate that the improvement amounts to between one and two grades' increase. They did not calculate what this might mean for primary age levels, but the implications are clear.

The resulting lengthy article was published in an academic journal (Black and Wiliam, 1998), and received national and international interest over the findings. That interest is still growing, as many countries are now finding out about the impact of formative assessment as a result of Black and Wiliam's trawl. Unfortunately, the very people who most need to know about this research, the teachers, are often the last to know – a flaw in the way in which research is often disseminated. Accordingly Black and Wiliam produced a digest of the article, entitled *Inside the Black Box*, which summarised the key findings. This was followed by *Assessment for Learning: Beyond the Black Box*, written by the Assessment Reform Group.

The purpose of these little books was to begin to bullet-point the conditions for success in the classroom, making them more accessible to teachers. Both digests give schools ideal material to use for parent communication and in policies, as they consist of many summary statements. My own work with teachers, including various research projects, aims to flesh out and define in more practical terms what formative assessment actually looks like in the classroom.

Bringing together so many studies led to the identification of clear themes. However, one theme emerged which Black and Wiliam saw as the key to successful learning: the importance of **high self-esteem**. This is dealt with in depth towards the end of this book – because the theme of self-esteem recurs throughout, so the threads are brought together as a kind of finale.

The key findings from Black and Wiliam's research are reproduced here:

6 *The research indicates that improving learning through assessment depends on five, deceptively simple, key factors:*

■ *the provision of effective feedback to pupils;*

■ *the active involvement of pupils in their own learning;*

■ *adjusting teaching to take account of the results of assessment;*

■ *a recognition of the profound influence assessment has on the motivation and self-esteem of pupils, both of which are crucial influences on learning;*

■ *the need for pupils to be able to assess themselves and understand how to improve.* 9

(page 4)

This was further broken down to include:

6 ■ *sharing learning goals with pupils,*

■ *involving pupils in self-assessment,*

■ *providing feedback which leads to pupils recognising their next steps and how to take them,*

■ *underpinned by confidence that every student can improve.* 9

(page 7)

The inhibiting factors identified included:

6 ■ *A tendency for teachers to assess quantity of work and presentation rather than the quality of learning;*

■ *greater attention given to marking and grading, much of it tending to lower the self-esteem of pupils, rather than to provide advice for improvement;*

■ *a strong emphasis on comparing pupils with each other which demoralises the less successful learners;*

■ *teachers' feedback to pupils often serves managerial and social purposes rather than helping them to learn more effectively.* 🍳

(page 5)<br>(Assessment Reform Group, 1999)

The picture painted appears quite bleak, but these strategies have given teachers a way forward. The current context in primary education in England is that government targets *must* be met. This has led to a classic 'high-stakes' testing culture, because the measure used is the number of Level 4s achieved in Key Stage 2 tests. Inevitably, as with all high-stakes testing, this has led to a narrowing of the curriculum and frequent teaching to the test, especially in Year 6. Ironically, if the national emphasis were on *formative* assessment, and if funding reinforced that emphasis, the government targets would probably be met via formative strategies being universally applied in our classrooms. It is by good teaching and learning that standards rise, not by summative or short-term measures to boost attainment – as has been proven by the Black and Wiliam research trawl.

The current OFSTED Handbook reflects the new emphasis on formative assessment in its key paragraph on assessment:

❛ **Do teachers assess pupils' work thoroughly and use assessments to help and encourage pupils to overcome difficulties?**

*Your judgements about teachers' assessment of their pupils should focus on how well teachers look for gains in learning, gaps in knowledge and areas of misunderstanding, through their day-to-day work with pupils. This will include marking, questioning of individuals and plenary sessions. Clues to the effectiveness of formative assessment are how well the teachers listen and respond to pupils, encourage and, where appropriate, praise them, recognise and handle misconceptions, build on their responses and steer them towards **clearer** understanding. Effective teachers encourage pupils to judge the success of their own work and set targets* *for improvement. They will take full account of the targets set out in individual education plans for pupils with special educational needs.* **9**

(*Handbook for Inspecting Primary and Nursery Schools,*
OFSTED, 2000)

We need both summative *and* formative assessment, not one or the other, because they both fulfil different, parallel purposes, as the gardening analogy shows. Making clear the difference between these purposes is of prime importance in helping teachers understand what is important and when each should be used. I recommend that assessment policies are divided into two sections, describing firstly the summative measures in place in the school and secondly formative strategies.

# Summative assessment

Current practice tends to consist of the following:

- baseline testing on school entry;
- statutory end-of-key-stage tests;
- non-statutory 'optional' tests;
- commercially produced tests, if chosen by the school;
- school and class tests, created by teachers;
- end-of-key-stage Teacher Assessment levels;
- end-of-year levels or sub-levels for individual children, currently tracked to see whether children are in line with projected targets for Year 6;
- any other summative information about performance in the school.

# Formative assessment

Practice drawn from the research base tends to consist of the following:

- clarifying learning intentions at the planning stage, as a condition for formative assessment to take place in the classroom (*chapter 1*);

- sharing learning intentions at beginnings of lessons (*chapter 2*);

- involving children in self-evaluation against learning intentions (*chapter 3*);

- focusing oral and written feedback around the learning intentions of lessons and tasks (*chapter 4*);

- organising individual target setting so that children's achievement is based on previous achievement as well as aiming for the next level up (ipsative referencing) (*chapter 5*);

- appropriate questioning (*chapter 6*);

- raising children's self-esteem via the language of the classroom and the ways in which achievement is celebrated (*chapter 8*).

# *1* Planning

In order to carry out formative assessment strategies in the classroom, the **learning intentions** of lessons need to be as clear as possible. As can be seen by the list of formative assessment 'ingredients' at the end of the Introduction, the learning intention is the heart of formative assessment, and needs to be made clear at the planning stage if teachers are to find formative assessment manageable.

The single most important element of planning, therefore – from long- to short-term – is the clarity of learning intentions.

## Long-term planning

Most schools have curriculum frameworks set in place, which need only occasional tinkering. This framework is the 'structure' plan which shows who covers what and when throughout the school, in order to ensure breadth, balance and coverage.

## Medium-term planning

The medium-term stage has undergone a number of changes and developments during the last few years, brought about mainly by the introduction of the National Literacy and Numeracy Strategies and the Qualifications & Curriculum Authority (QCA) Schemes of Work, which have been widely taken up. Whereas there used to be a clear difference between teachers' medium-term plans and schemes of work, there has been considerable merging of the two.

**LINGFIELD PRIMARY SCHOOL – LONG TERM PLAN** — AUTUMN TERM / SECOND HALF TERM — YEAR 6

| SUBJECT | WEEK 1 | WEEK 2 | WEEK 3 | WEEK 4 | WEEK 5 | WEEK 6 | WEEK 7 | WEEK 8 |
|---|---|---|---|---|---|---|---|---|
| ENGLISH | DISCUSSION TEXT (TL2 16,18) CONNECTING WORDS (SL2 4C) SPELLING (WL2 8) | CLASSIC FICTION RIKKI TIKI TAVI (TL1 1,2,6A TL2 1,2) SPELLING MNEMONICS (WL 4B) COMPREHENSION ASSESSMENT | EXPLANATION TEXT (TL3 15,17) IMPERSONAL VOICE (SL2 2) SPELLING WORDS WITHIN WORDS( WL 3A) | STRUCTURE OF SHORT STORIES 9TL3 15,17) SPEECH SPELLING UNSTRESSED VOWELS (WL2 4C) | STORY POETRY (TL2 9) ADAPTING TEXT (SL1 1E) SPELLING RULES (WL2 3B) | WRITING WORKSHOP TYPES OF TEXT 9TL1 1) SPELLING PROVERBS (WL 2 6) | PRINT AND FILM 9TL1 1) ASSESSMENT | |
| MATHS | AREA AND PERIMETER (SURREY WK 10) | MULTIPLICATION AND ASSESSMENT (SURREY WK 12 & 13) | | DIVISION (SURREY WK 14) | PLACE VALUE & DECIMALS (SURREY WK 14) ROCKS (SC3 1D) | PERCENTAGES (SURREY WK 16) DESIGN EXP TO PROVE GIVEN RESULTS(SC1) | MATHS CLINIC ASSESSMENT | |
| SCIENCE | PHYSICAL CHANGE & REVERSIBILITY (SC3 2D) | | SOLUBILITY EXPERIMENT (SC1) | | | | | |
| D.T | DESIGNING & MAKING MOVING TOY (SCHOOL SCHEME OF WORK) | | | | | | | |
| GEOGRAPHY | KNOWLEDGE AND UNDERSTANDING ABOUT PLACES- WHAT IS A TOWN? (G 1A, 2C) | HOW DO TOWNS WORK?( G 2B, 5B) | WHY DO TOWNS DEVELOP? ( G 3E, 5A) | WHAT MAKES A CITY? ( G 3A,D) | WHAT DO YOU KNOW ABOUT CITIES AROUND THE WORLD? (G 2C,3A) | HOW DOES A CITY FUNCTION OVER 24 HRS? (G 2D) | | |
| MUSIC ( UNIT 17 QCA SCHEME) | EXPLORING ROUNDS COMBINING PITCHED NOTES | SINGING ROUNDS IN 2 PARTS | | | REHERSE AND | PERFORMANCE | | |
| R.E | THE TRINITY – LOOKING AT HYMNS INVOLVING TRINITY | | | | | | | |
| I.C.T | BROWSING THE WEB | SEARCH ENGINES | | | | | | |
| P.E | GYMNASTICS (UNIT 6 QCA) HOCKEY (INVASION GAMES | | | | | | | |
| P.S.H.E | BEHAVIOR- CONSEQUENCE | | | | | | | |
| FRENCH | FRUIT & VEG | | | | | | | |

**LINGFIELD PRIMARY SCHOOL – LONG TERM PLAN** — AUTUMN TERM / SECOND HALF TERM — YEAR 2

| SUBJECT | WEEK 1 | WEEK 2 | WEEK 3 | WEEK 4 | WEEK 5 | WEEK 6 | WEEK 7 |
|---|---|---|---|---|---|---|---|
| ENGLISH 7 hrs refs: NLP Y2 T1 | Continuous: W11,12 S1,3,4 T1,2, 9 T13,14 to read simple written instructions, to note key structural features (non-fiction) | T15-18 S6 to write simple instructions, use models to organise instructions, use diagrams, use appropriate register | T8,12 to collect and categorise poems, to use simple poetry structures to write new lines | | T3 to be aware of differences between spoken and written language T5 to identify and discuss reasons for events in stories linked to plot S5 to begin to use capitalisation in own writing | | assessment |
| | W3 ar,oa short 00 | W3ou, ow | W3oi, oy | W3 air, ere, ear, are | W3 or, oor, aw, au W7 ed | W3 er ir ur W7 ed | |
| speaking and listening ref NC | W5, 6, 9 to read, write and spell HF words from List 1 W10 vocabulary extension: new words from reading linked to particular topics (cross curricular) | | | | | | |
| MATHS 4 hrs Refs: NNP Oral and mental | All of En 1 covered through all subjects plus specific topics in PSHE and Drama (below) Unit 8 counting and properties of numbers reasoning about numbers | Unit 9 Place value, ordering, and understanding + and | Units 10, 11 Understanding multiplication and division Money problems fractions | | Units 12,13 Measures and time, including problems Handling data | | Unit 14 assessment |
| | Bridging 10 | Money problems Addition in any order | Counting 1, 2, 10 | Number bonds to 20 | doubles | Halves/doubles | |
| SCIENCE 2 hrs | Sc4 : 3 a,b light and dark | | | | | | |
| ICT 1/2 hr 'taught' plus paired follow up | 1 c retrieve information, 2a to use text, images 3a presenting information in a variety of forms | | | | | | |
| HISTORY 1 hr | 6d past events from British History Gunpowder plot | 6c significant people Isaac Newton | 6c significant people Monet | | | | |
| GEOGRAPHY DT 2 hrs ART 2hrs | 1a,b, 4a visual and tactile elements 5 a,b,c, breadth of study Light and dark | | Line and tone | | Form and space | | Card making |

**LINGFIELD PRIMARY SCHOOL – LONG TERM PLAN** — TERM 1 / FIRST HALF TERM — YEAR R

| SUBJECT | WEEK 1 | WEEK 2 | WEEK 3 | WEEK 4 | WEEK 5 | WEEK 6 | WEEK 7 | WEEK 8 |
|---|---|---|---|---|---|---|---|---|
| Mathematical Development | Numbers 1-5 FM 1 N1 Focus – No. 1 | No. 2 | No. 3 | No. 4 | No. 5 | Numbers 6-10 Revision of counting 1 to 1 up to 5 FM 1,3 N3 | Shape 2D shapes – squares and circles FM 9 N9 | |
| Language and Literacy | Introduction to 'Big Books' and Early literacy Skills ( title, author, print direction, difference between words and pictures, words and letters, print carries meaning) , recognising own name TL 1a,b,c,d SL 3, FL 14, 15 Vocabulary work WL 10, TL 8 Speaking and Listening skills ( sharing, discussing, listening and responding to stories/poems, role play) | | | Phonic work WL2a,b,c 3a,b,c FL12 FL 1,2,3,4,5,6,7,8,9,10 Writing skills (correct pencil grip, letter formation, name writing) WL8,12,13,14 TL11b,d,e 12a SL4 FL19 | Sequencing a familiar story TL7,9 FL5,9 | Guided writing TL12c,d 13 | Using a dictionary and list writing TL1a,b 11a WL3c, FL16 | |
| Personal and Social Development | Class rules P.E. rules PSD8,9,10,12 | | Turn taking PSD8 | Reasons for paying attention PSD3 | Helping others PSD4 | Introduction to non-fiction texts TL1b,c 6 FL15 Harvest Celebration PSD5,13 | Poppy Day PSD5 | |
| Knowledge and Understanding of the World | Recognition of basic colours KU1 | | | | Food KU1 | Vegetables KU1 | Shops KU9 | |
| Creative Development | Use of paint and brushes CD1 | Mixing colours CD1 | Using different papers CD3 | Printing CD1 | | Tasting KU1,3 | | |
| | Clap rhythms of familiar rhymes CD2 | | Music and Movement CD4 | Wax resist CD1 | | Food rhythms CD2 | | |
| Physical Development | Safety rules in P.E. PD1,3 | Small apparatus PD6 | Understand body changes in P.E. PD5 | | 'through' small apparatus PD7 | | | |
| | | | Music and Movement PD2,3 | | | | | |

*Fig. 1.1 Examples of long-term plans*

Many schools now use the QCA schemes of work as medium-term plans, saving themselves more work. However, there is a serious point to be made about a situation where teaching activities are 'set in stone' through printed material. The implication is that this plan should not really change, except for minor modification. Yet whether activities are appropriate and fulfil learning intentions should be in constant question. Although it might sound pedantic, it would create a healthier psychological starting point if the schemes of work were printed with enough space under each activity for a teacher to start again and rethink the whole thing. Deciding to change activities as a result of how things are going in the classroom is, as OFSTED puts it, *'using assessment information to inform planning'*.

Many schools now use the Literacy and Numeracy Frameworks themselves as medium-term plans, highlighting the coverage for each term, sometimes cutting and pasting this on to separate sheets. The activity suggestions are then drawn from school schemes of work or, more commonly, from commercial schemes.

**Some key points about medium-term plans/schemes of work:**

■ Learning intentions should be defined at this stage and reworked to make them as unambiguous and clear as possible, including bracketed 'example' statements wherever necessary to illuminate unclear aspects – e.g. *'To be able to introduce a character (e.g. attitude to others, hobbies, sense of humour, general personality)'*.

■ Learning intentions should be seen as a menu for the half-term rather than a list to be followed in exact order.

■ Because of the nature of knowledge, concepts and skills, learning intentions cannot possibly have equal weighting in the amount of time allocated to each – *concepts* are likely to need more time for deeper learning than, say, the acquisition of *knowledge*.

■ Aim for as few activities as possible to be linked with grouped learning intentions, rather than one-to-one correspondence.

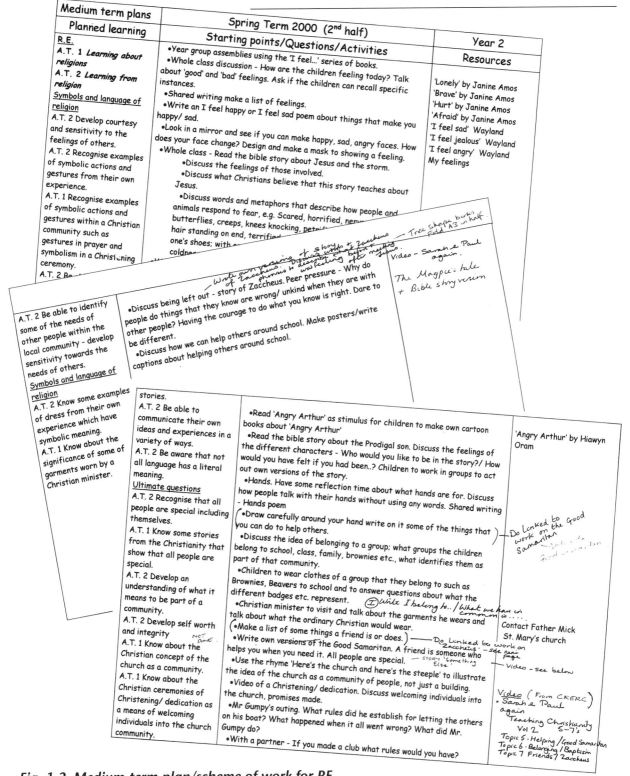

| Medium term plans | | Year 2 |
| --- | --- | --- |
| **Planned learning** | **Spring Term 2000 (2nd half)** | |
| R.E. | **Starting points/Questions/Activities** | **Resources** |

**R.E.**
**A.T. 1** *Learning about religions*
**A.T. 2** *Learning from religion*
<u>Symbols and language of religion</u>
A.T. 2 Develop courtesy and sensitivity to the feelings of others.
A.T. 2 Recognise examples of symbolic actions and gestures from their own experience.
A.T. 1 Recognise examples of symbolic actions and gestures within a Christian community such as gestures in prayer and symbolism in a Christening ceremony.
A.T. 2 Be...

• Year group assemblies using the 'I feel...' series of books.
• Whole class discussion – How are the children feeling today? Talk about 'good' and 'bad' feelings. Ask if the children can recall specific instances.
• Shared writing make a list of feelings.
• Write an I feel happy or I feel sad poem about things that make you happy/ sad.
• Look in a mirror and see if you can make happy, sad, angry faces. How does your face change? Design and make a mask to showing a feeling.
• Whole class – Read the bible story about Jesus and the storm.
  • Discuss the feelings of those involved.
  • Discuss what Christians believe that this story teaches about Jesus.
  • Discuss words and metaphors that describe how people and animals respond to fear, e.g. Scared, horrified, nerv... butterflies, creeps, knees knocking, petri... hair standing on end, terrified... one's shoes; with...
coldness...

'Lonely' by Janine Amos
'Brave' by Janine Amos
'Hurt' by Janine Amos
'Afraid' by Janine Amos
'I feel sad' Wayland
'I feel jealous' Wayland
'I feel angry' Wayland
My feelings

*(handwritten)* Write our own versions of shrugs of Zacchaeus – Discuss words that... Zacchaeus was feeling after meeting... Tree shape books Fold A3 in half.
*(handwritten)* Video - Sarah & Paul again.
*(handwritten)* The Magpie's tale + Bible story version

A.T. 2 Be able to identify some of the needs of other people within the local community – develop sensitivity towards the needs of others.
<u>Symbols and language of religion</u>
A.T. 2 Know some examples of dress from their own experience which have symbolic meaning.
A.T. 1 Know about the significance of some of garments worn by a Christian minister.

• Write own versions of story of Zacchaeus. Peer pressure – Why do people do things that they know are wrong/ unkind when they are with other people? Having the courage to do what you know is right. Dare to be different.
• Discuss how we can help others around school. Make posters/write captions about helping others around school.

stories.
A.T. 2 Be able to communicate their own ideas and experiences in a variety of ways.
A.T. 2 Be aware that not all language has a literal meaning.
<u>Ultimate questions</u>
A.T. 2 Recognise that all people are special including themselves.
A.T. 1 Know some stories from the Christianity that show that all people are special.
A.T. 2 Develop an understanding of what it means to be part of a community.
A.T. 2 Develop self worth and integrity *(handwritten: NOT DONE)*
A.T. 1 Know about the Christian concept of the church as a community.
A.T. 1 Know about the Christian ceremonies of Christening/ dedication as a means of welcoming individuals into the church community.

• Read 'Angry Arthur' as stimulus for children to make own cartoon books about 'Angry Arthur'
• Read the bible story about the Prodigal son. Discuss the feelings of the different characters – Who would you like to be in the story?/ How would you have felt if you had been..? Children to work in groups to act out own versions of the story.
• Hands. Have some reflection time about what hands are for. Discuss how people talk with their hands without using any words. Shared writing – Hands poem
• Draw carefully around your hand write on it some of the things that you can do to help others.
• Discuss the idea of belonging to a group; what groups the children belong to school, class, family, brownies etc., what identifies them as part of that community.
• Children to wear clothes of a group that they belong to such as Brownies, Beavers to school and to answer questions about what the different badges etc. represent. *(handwritten)* (I) Write I belong to.. / What we have in common is.....
• Christian minister to visit and talk about the garments he wears and talk about what the ordinary Christian would wear.
• Make a list of some things a friend is or does. *(handwritten)* Do Linked to work on Zacchaeus - see next page
• Write own versions of the Good Samaritan. A friend is someone who helps you when you need it. All people are special. *(handwritten)* STORY Something Else
• Use the rhyme 'Here's the church and here's the steeple' to illustrate the idea of the church as a community of people, not just a building.
• Video of a Christening/ dedication. Discuss welcoming individuals into the church, promises made.
• Mr Gumpy's outing. What rules did he establish for letting the others on his boat? What happened when it all went wrong? What did Mr. Gumpy do?
• With a partner – If you made a club what rules would you have?

'Angry Arthur' by Hiawyn Oram

*(handwritten)* Do Linked to Good work on the Good Samaritan

Contact Father Mick
St. Mary's church
*(handwritten)* Video - see below

*(handwritten)* Video (From CRERC) · Sarah & Paul again Teaching Christianity Vol 2   5–7's
Topic 5 - Helping / Good Samaritan
Topic 6 - Belonging / Baptism
Topic 7 Friends / Zacchaeus

*Fig. 1.2. Medium-term plan/scheme of work for RE*

■ Consider the learning intentions column in the medium-term plan first, when creating next week's plan. Then decide whether activities should change in the light of your understanding of the children's understanding.

# Short-term planning

Short-term plans usually consist of three documents: a Numeracy plan, a Literacy plan and a plan for everything else.

As with medium-term or Scheme of Work planning, the most important feature of a short-term plan is the clarity of learning intentions. These should be shown for every lesson, session or area of provision, so that the focus of the teacher's thinking – both in planning the week's activities and in teaching – is the learning which will take place. Sharing learning intentions with pupils is much easier if the first point of reference in a weekly plan is the learning intention for each lesson.

Sometimes, in breaking learning intentions down at the short-term stage, they can inadvertently mutate into activities rather than learning intentions. For example:

*'To understand the effect of banana production on the banana producers'* is really an **activity** description.

The **learning intention** should be: *'To understand the effect of production on the producers.'*

The learning intention here is about understanding the effect of any production on the producers. The teacher has decided to use bananas as a context for that learning intention, but it is not bananas we really want the children to know about. We are simply using that context as a vehicle for enabling the children to understand the learning intention. If we share the learning intention with the word *banana* in it, at the beginning of the lesson, the children will believe it is important that they know about bananas. The *'production/producers'* learning intention, however, will encourage children to think about how all production affects its producers. In fact, the plenary of the lesson should develop the lesson away from bananas in order to make this important connection. The activity instructions will spell out the banana context, so children will be clear about what is expected of them. With a clear learning intention, they are also clear about what they are really supposed to be learning.

## Consistency

Many schools have tried to achieve consistency in short-term planning by insisting that all teachers use the same-size piece of paper. A better approach seems to be to decide jointly on a **format**, but then to print the plan in different sizes, so that everyone's handwriting and writing needs are met.

The **ingredients** of the short-term plan need to be consistent from teacher to teacher. These are probably obvious: for each lesson or space of time, the following ingredients should be shown, in as succinct a way as possible: *the learning intention for the lesson, the activity, how it will be differentiated and, finally, a space for assessment jottings to inform future planning.*

## Assessment to inform future planning

Since 1994, the statutory requirements for ongoing record keeping have been stated in the QCA *Assessment and Reporting* booklets. The statement has remained the same for some years, that:

> *In retaining evidence and keeping records, schools should be guided by what is both useful and manageable in planning future work.*

In 2000, the statement contained the further advice to read QCA's *Keeping Track* document. This is a useful guide, showing ways in which schools have recorded pupil achievement. The paragraph about short-term planning explains:

> *Day-to-day assessment is a reflection of the extent to which pupils are achieving the objectives set out in lesson plans. Teachers routinely observe features of their pupils' learning, but much of this is not recorded. Adjustments to plans for*

*the next day or the next lesson will usually take account of how far the teaching has helped some or all pupils achieve the learning objectives. Occasionally it helps to annotate lesson plans, especially if a teacher needs to return to a concept with a particular group of pupils. Teachers' own notes need only be as detailed as is helpful.* **9**

Under 'Teachers' ongoing records' they say:

**6** *Teachers can review the rate of progress by looking at work in pupils' folders or exercise books and by the marks in their record books. They can then use this to adjust day-to-day teaching and plan further work. One way to improve manageability would be to make a note only of those pupils who achieve significantly above or below the expected outcomes of a task.* **9**

(*Keeping Track*, QCA, 1999)

Most short-term plans have assessment or evaluation columns, but these are often not completed or consist of '*so what?*' comments (comments on how well children did – such as '*Green group did very well/Yellow group enjoyed this*' – which are not useful for the teacher in future planning or in any sense). Comments about lack of understanding are more useful, because this can be used in future planning. However, if there will be no opportunity to follow up misunderstandings, there seems little point in writing them down. If ongoing assessment is to be worthwhile, it needs to focus on extreme achievement or extreme lack of achievement against the learning intention, manifested as brief jottings about *what needs to happen next* in planning.

## Formats and design

Many formats are possible for weekly/daily planning, but the following pointers should be taken into account, whatever the design:

*1*   Make it clear that, once teachers have included the basic ingredients in the plan, they do not need to fill all the blank space! Since many teachers have been word-processing weekly plans, more and more seems to be written, almost because there is more space to fill with typed writing. Teachers need to be reassured that they do not *have* to write every detail of a lesson, or their energies are taken up by planning rather than thinking about learning and preparation.

2    Aim for streamlining Literacy and Numeracy plans in the future, as teachers become more familiar with the content – at present, they take up most of the planning time. Many schools are now word-processing weekly Literacy and Numeracy plans in order to create a bank of weekly plans with associated Big Books and so on for the following year. (See Chapter 3, on self-evaluation, for ways of cutting down what is written for the plenary.)

3    Design the plan so that **the learning intentions are written, individually, wherever the activity is written**, rather than in a bank or box at the top or bottom of the plan. This makes a significant difference to teachers, because the first point of reference then, for every lesson, is the learning. When objectives are written in a 'bank' or box somewhere on the plan, it is too easy to give them only a cursory glance and become focused on what the children are going *to do* rather than what they are going *to learn*.

4    Instead of a column entitled 'assessment' or 'evaluation', entitle it **'Notes for future planning'**. Then every teacher is clear about the *purpose* of assessment notes on the plan: it is not an evaluation of the lesson (unnecessary) or notes on how well children did, but the place for specific notes about what needs to change – tomorrow or next week.

5    In monitoring individual teachers' plans, it is a good idea for headteachers, for a few weeks, to highlight those aspects which really do inform future planning and cross out comments which do not, so that teachers can see what they do *not* need to write. Teachers can then understand more fully the idea of assessment being used to *inform* planning.

The audience for the short-term plan is, firstly, the people who will be working with the children during that week. The plan should *not* be written with an OFSTED inspector in mind – unless, of course, the school is currently under inspection! Inspectors of course need more detail than would be usual if they are going to judge the quality of a lesson through observation, but that level of detail is unsustainable during the rest of the year.

As already stated, plans should be as succinct as possible, written with abbreviations or bullet points to save time wherever possible.

Many teachers also display a copy of the short-term plan on the classroom wall every Monday, for children to see what will be happening during the week. Because it is possible that activities will change in the light of assessment information, it is more focusing for children if this plan simply shows the learning intentions for the week.

A *good* short-term plan will look messy by Friday, because that is the proof that a teacher has been *'using assessment information to inform planning'*. There could be crossings out, lessons extended or moved, reminders and so on, indicating that the plan is being used and is a *dynamic* instrument. Plans which are still pristine on Friday invariably indicate that the plan has been completed for monitoring purposes only and teachers' real plans are written elsewhere – unless, that is, the plans have been created on word-processor, when changes can be made on a day-by-day basis, with no evidence of the changes made. This is an inevitable consequence of technology!

## The future

Once the Literacy and Numeracy frameworks are firmly embedded in teachers' minds, it might be possible to limit the extent of planning and return to a 'week to view' plan. The *enlarged timetable style* short-term format is very popular with teachers, because it more closely resembles the progression of a week than separate subject plans. Two sides of A3 paper should eventually be possible (in some schools it already is), with each lesson shown as a timetable box, where all the key ingredients are shown: learning intention, what and how, and a space for assessment jottings for future planning.

Bearing in mind the central importance of knowing the learning intention of each lesson, and ensuring quality learning activities, we need to move towards a culture where teachers can divert their energies into the practice of and

**Sheet 1 (top):**

LINGFIELD SHORT TERM PLANNING

| | | Adult Support | Assessment / evaluation |

TERM 1a (AUTUMN) SPRING SUMMER 200   WEEK 3

Activities

Learning intentions

SCIENCE
To know how muscles work.
× Elastic band demonstration - (working in pairs)
Cloze sheet on key facts.
× Musles fact sheet - how to use sheet to produce one.
" ✓ (Need card for band demon.)

ART
To know who Klee was
To produce a wax scrape.
Oral work on Klee.
model stages × base colours × black out × scrape.
" ✓

GEOGRAPHY
To produce a weather forcast
× Identify regions of the UK make compass.
× Match forcast to region.
" To be completed Mon. am.

HISTORY
Copy topic sheet.
...retrieve
" ✓ (See list)

---

**Sheet 2 (middle) — NUMERACY:**

TERM 1a (AUTUMN) SPRING SUMMER 200
WEEK 3

LINGFIELD SHORT TERM PLANNING - NUMERACY

| | MONDAY | TUESDAY | WEDNESDAY | THURSDAY | FRIDAY | VOCABULARY |
|---|---|---|---|---|---|---|
| Learning intentions | | | | | | extend to next week. Gen. move w/ ball. Harry o/E |
| oral/mental | See NLS week 4  -1,10,100, 1000 from a number. | TEST +/- 1,10,100, 1000  Jordan Micha Charm Daniel | TEST 2,3,5,10 tables | 3x table (number line) | Counting on in 3s  Fractions of length test (use sheet) | charm. Micha Ben Lucy Emmie Jordan  Retest on MON  v.gd: Emily, Ben. v.gd response in gen. |
| whole class | Length, units and abbrevia-tions. Using a ruler | Relationship // units, eg. 10mm = 1cm | → Extend eg. 30mm = 3cm (Recap using a ruler) | Fractions of length (½,¼,¹⁄₁₀) measuring around | Define perim. ↳ model on board + common error (only ½) Measuring |
| Activities / outcomes  L1 | | GINN 4 (est.) | | | | |
| L2 | GINN | | | | | |
| L3 | Obje... m EXT | | | | | |
| IEP | | | | | | |
| Adult support | | | | | | |
| plenary | Chec... | | | | | |
| assessment / evaluation | Eye... | | | | | |

---

**Sheet 3 (bottom) — LITERACY:**

TERM 1a (AUTUMN) SPRING SUMMER 200
WEEK 3

LINGFIELD SHORT TERM PLANNING - LITERACY

| | MONDAY | TUESDAY | WEDNESDAY | THURSDAY | FRIDAY | VOCABULARY inc spelling |
|---|---|---|---|---|---|---|
| Learning intentions | To recognise key features in historical playscripts →  To know where sp. mrks. go. | To change a story into a play. | To identify verbs and adverbs. To write clearly and joined | To use commas to indicate pause in WR | → To know the main features of a play. To write a short play. | |
| Word / sentence level | Tch. play to story Excuses, excuses ↳ format of a play, text as orally. | The Working Children  " | slowly (by James Reeves) Identify verbs. | The Working Children focus on × pauses × commas | Model WR a scene from a play. | |
| Text level | Model changing the play to narrative form focus "speech mrks" | model changing narrative to a play | ×verb endings (tense) ×adverbs. | Comma sheet (Lit ⑩) | PAIRS ↓ | |
| Activities / outcomes | change "excuses..." to narrative. | Mallory Cox (pg.14), Angel of Nitshill (EXT). | Copy out descriptions (A4) | Comma sheet (EXT) Verb sheet | ↓ (Jordan + Micha commas) | |
| Group: Guided WR  IEP | | | | | | |
| Adult support | HN  Part each | | | | | |
| plenary | Read stories out. | Read plays out.  " | Jordan, Daniel, Charm. speechmarks. Class Story  spot verbs | Jordan + Ben handwriting (same sheet) | Play w/ BG. | |
| assessment / evaluation | Jordan Daniel Charm. } not full sp. mrks. Wed. | ✓ | ✓ Mitchell - start joing more | Mark work (comma card) ✓ Jordan, Micha careful with unnec. commas | Read plays out. ✓ | |

*Fig. 1.3 Example of a short-term plan (weekly/daily) covering three sides of A4 paper*

preparation for *teaching and learning* rather than hours of over-detailed planning. Chapter 7 in this book explores the ways in which monitoring of planning can reflect these aims.

## INSET ideas

1. In a staff meeting, ask pairs of teachers to look at current medium-term plans and/or schemes of work and annotate the learning intentions to make them clearer.
2. Subject coordinators can do the same, inserting bracketed 'for example' comments beside unclear words.
3. Word-process medium-term plans so that teachers do not have to write out learning intentions from one plan to another.
4. Give input about short-term planning and suggest two or three new formats as outlined in this chapter. Ask staff to trial these over the next few weeks.
5. Have a feedback meeting and ask for staff views: focus on manageability, usefulness, clarity of learning intentions and appropriate assessment jottings.
6. Keep the plans under review.

# 2 Sharing learning intentions

The first 'active' element of formative assessment in the classroom is the sharing of learning intentions with children. A significant feature of effective feedback in many studies is the importance of informing children of the learning objective of a task (see, for example, Crooks, 1988; Hillocks, 1986; Ames and Ames, 1984; Butler, 1988). Since the onset of OFSTED inspections, primary teachers in England are expected to inform children of task learning objectives, and children are typically questioned during inspections to confirm th[...] lesson. The Literacy and [...] expect teachers to share l[...] beginnings of lessons.

*[handwritten note: Whole school approach explain in a way that makes sense to teacher & pupils.]*

Research shows that chil[...] oriented if they know the learning intention of the task, but they are also able to make better decisions about *how to go about the task*. Without the learning intention, children are merely victims of the teacher's whim. It is vital, therefore, that learning intentions should be shared with children for every lesson, not just Literacy and Numeracy. Children are likely, otherwise, to assume that other areas of the curriculum do not have learning goals and will be confused by not being given the same amount of information for some tasks as for others.

Learning intentions about the curriculum are sometimes known as 'mastery goals', defined by Carole Ames (1992):

❛ *With a mastery goal, individuals are oriented toward developing new skills, trying to understand their work, improving their level of competence, or achieving a sense of mastery based on self-referenced standards. Compatible with this goal construct is Brophy's (1983) description of a "motivation to learn" whereby individuals are focusing on mastering and understanding content and demonstrating a willingness to engage in the process of learning.* **9**

The sharing of a learning intention is, however, more complex than simply repeating what is in the teacher's plan. It is also only the first step in the processes of formative assessment, leading to pupil self-evaluation and teacher or peer feedback after the work is completed. In order for the learning intention to be shared effectively, it needs to be clear and unambiguous, so that the teacher can explain it in a way which makes sense to her and the children.

Secondly, the task has to **match** the learning intention for the children to have a chance of fulfilling it. Thirdly, the learning intention has the greatest impact on children's understanding of the task and their progress if it includes **success criteria** as well as the learning intention itself and fourthly it needs to be the main focus of **feedback** (see Chapter 4).

# Developing a 'learning culture' in the school

The following strategies have been tried and tested in many schools across the country over several years: they are continually developing, as teachers find out more about involving children in their learning.

*1* **Make sure the learning objective of a task is clear.** These may be derived from the National Curriculum Programmes of Study, the QCA Schemes of Work, the Literacy or Numeracy objectives, teachers' own breakdowns of the statutory objectives or teachers' and children's own learning intentions, when extending the curriculum beyond the bare minimum of the National Curriculum.

*2* **It is best if there is a whole-school approach** to and launch of the sharing of learning intentions for every lesson. Children need to be told, preferably by the head in an assembly, that *from now on they will not only be told what we want them to do for every lesson, but also what we hope they will* *be learning. And if we forget to do this, we want them to remind us* (they do!). This needs to be reiterated by the teachers in their own classrooms. Children have then been given a basic expectation about their rights as a learner.

3 **Teachers need to separate the task instructions clearly from the learning intention and success criteria**, or children can begin their work without knowing clearly the difference between **what you want them to *do*** and **what you want them to *learn***. For many lessons where children will be asked to do some independent or group work, rather than engage in discussion, *it is more effective to begin with the activity instructions*, rather than the learning intention.

Children often first need to be 'capture' lesson, by the context and your introd' Then the learning intention becomes jigsaw for them to be able to focus ap they have been asked to do. If teache learning intention as the first words *morning we are going to be looking at h... paragraphs'*), even the most diligent chil .kely to feel jaded. Given an interesting passage as a starting point, however, most children will be comparatively motivated. Clearly, there will be some situations where it makes more sense to *start* with the learning intention, because that helps make sense of the activity instructions. In many cases, however, the learning intention makes no sense if given too early, before the children have heard the activity context – especially if it is a new area of learning.

4 The learning intention seems to be more effective if, once stated – in 'child-speak' if the children would not understand its original form – it is then followed by an **invitation to create the success criteria**: *'How will we know we've achieved this?'*.

## For example

> **Activity instructions** involve asking children, in pairs, to count piles of objects and match them with numeral cards.
>
> **Learning intention** shared is expressed **'We are learning to say the numbers we write down, from 0 to 10'** (child-speak version of *'To recognise numbers to 10'*).

Children are then asked *'How will we know we have done/learnt that?'*, resulting in a quick (no more than a minute) brainstorm to agree success criteria. For many lessons this will simply be one statement, but by the end of Key Stage 2 a list of criteria might be generated. For some lessons the teacher might tell the children the success criteria.

**Success criteria** are established as *'So what we're looking for is that you can say the names of all these numbers'*.

## The purpose of the success criteria

The purpose of the success criteria or *'What we're looking for'* is to make children absolutely sure about what is in the teacher's mind as the criteria for judging their work. Too often children know the learning intention, but not how the teacher is going to judge their performance. A learning intention of *'Using effective adjectives'*, for instance, does not give the children the marking criteria or how they will be judged.

The *'How will we know?'* needs to state exactly what the children and teacher will want to see. In this case, three alternatives might be: *'What you're looking for is that you have used at least five effective adjectives'*, or *'What you're looking for is that you have used at least four adjectives just before a noun'*, or *'What you're looking for is that you used at least four adjectives which describe the jungle.'*

## Inviting the children to create success criteria

After children have been told the learning intention, they can invariably suggest how the teacher – and they
elves – will know that this has been learnt or carried
hey now know the activity and the learning intention,
success criteria are heavily contextualised. However,
portance of inviting children to create the success
a in this way is that it involves them still further in
own learning. They are being asked, effectively, to link the learning intention with the task instructions. They then have to decide how the two are synthesised to create success criteria – a much more challenging learning experience than simply being *given* the information.

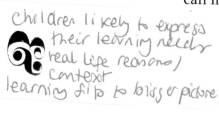

Children likely to express their learning needs (real life reasons) context
learning fits to bigger picture

They have even more of a stake in the learning process if they have been involved in the creation of success criteria and are more likely to be able to be self-evaluative as they are working, and questioning about the task as it evolves.

5   **Tell the children why they are learning this at all** – how it fits into the bigger picture. For instance, *'You are learning about the heart because it is important to know about how your body works/You are creating adjectives so that your writing will be more interesting/You are learning to say these numbers because you will need to do this in everyday life'*, etc. I call this the **'aside'** because it is generally too time-consuming to display, although some schools do this.

6   **The learning intention and success criteria need to be visually displayed** for every lesson (with the exception of hall or playground activities!). Making the visual display accessible to children is vital. Some schools have a wipe-clean chart (many variations of this are possible) to display the learning intention and success criteria as a character called **WALT** (for 'We Are Learning To...') with cartoon speech bubbles for the teacher to write in. An alternative design is a single character (an owl or suchlike) called WALT with two speech bubbles, one for *'We are learning to . . .'* and the other for *'How will you know you have achieved this?'* The text is permanent and the contents of the speech bubbles are wiped clean each time.

7   Ask children to **read aloud** the learning intention and success criteria (or WALT and *How will we know?/What we're looking for*). This is another way of making sure you have maximum attention from the class, exploiting different learning styles.

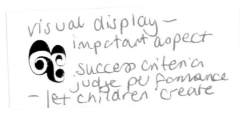

*Fig. 2.1 The learning intention and success criteria*

## Summary of steps

■ Clarify learning intentions at planning stage.

■ Make it an expectation for children.

■ Explain the learning intention, in 'child-speak' if necessary.

■ Invite children to say how we will know this has been done.

■ Write the success criterion or criteria.

■ The 'aside': say *why* this is an important thing to learn – the 'big picture'.

■ Get the children to read out the learning intention and success criteria.

**N.B.** The variations of characters and speech bubbles are simply tools for making the sharing of learning intentions accessible. What matters is the underlying principle: are children given access to the learning intention, success criteria and 'big picture'?

## *The power of the visual image*

It is only recently that I have fully realised the power of the words we write on flipcharts and whiteboards. In interviews with 72 children, in classes where I knew the teachers were sharing learning intentions verbally, I asked the children whether or not the teachers told them learning intentions. I rephrased this in several ways, even giving examples of learning intentions. All but the brightest children denied that they were being given learning intentions, although some did say that their teacher told them they were doing some activities 'for the SATs'.

I then asked the teachers to *display* learning intentions for eight weeks and re-interviewed the same children. The difference was astonishing. All children, across the ability range, talked about the 'learning intention', explaining how their teacher wrote it up on a board and even giving me examples of learning intentions from that day. Brighter children said that it helped them focus on the aspect in hand and not get distracted by other things. Less able children said that they looked up at the learning intention – and especially the success criteria – to remind themselves of what they were supposed to be doing! So it has different benefits for different abilities.

It is common to see activity instructions written for all to see in primary classrooms, giving a very clear message to children that the reason they come to school is to 'do activities'. Once *learning intentions* become the focus of display, children's language about lessons changes. They use the vocabulary of the learning intentions to describe their learning, to each other and to their parents, so a painting activity is likely to be described as *'We were learning to blend colours!'* rather than *'We painted rainbows'*.

This goes a long way towards creating a learning, rather than an activity, culture as the established ethos of the school, which encourages children to be active, self-evaluative learners, intrinsically rather than extrinsically motivated to learn and fulfil their potential.

## How should learning intentions and success criteria be displayed?

There are many ways of sharing learning intentions visually. Possibilities include:

- A wipe-clean whiteboard, with text written in permanent ink, or stuck on the wall next to the whiteboard, or on the whiteboard itself.

- A page on the flip chart, with text and speech bubbles, with the inserts for the speech bubbles written on A4 paper and tacked onto the bubbles for each lesson, torn down at the end of the lesson.

# Some examples of learning intentions and success criteria

(Remember: the children are invited to come up with the success criteria, although the teacher in some instances might think it better to create this herself because the context is too complex.)

---

**Learning intention in teacher's plan:** To explore narrative order and identify and map out the main stages of a story.

**Shared with children:**

**Learning intention:** *We are learning to order our own and other stories.*
**Success criteria:** *We will have ordered the story we looked at into our own story plan.*
**ASIDE (oral only):** *Ordering is an important skill in reading, writing and maths.*

---

**Learning intention in teacher's plan:** To be able to use and apply doubling and halving.

**Shared with children:**

**Learning intention:** *We are learning to use doubling and halving in everyday life.*
**Success criteria:** *We can show more than one way to double and halve numbers.*
**ASIDE (oral only):** *This will help you in everyday life, when shopping for two of the same thing, etc. . . .*

---

**Learning intention in teacher's plan:** To recognise numbers to 10.

**Shared with children:**

**Learning intention:** *We are learning to say or recognise the numbers we write down.*
**Success criteria:** *We can tell someone the names of all these numbers.*
**ASIDE (oral only):** *You'll need to know numbers on buses and doors, etc. . . .*

*Fig. 2.2 Learning intention and success criteria written on a whiteboard*

# Ways in which learning intention and success criteria might be written

*1*  There might be one learning intention but several success criteria, because the children are working in differentiated groups.

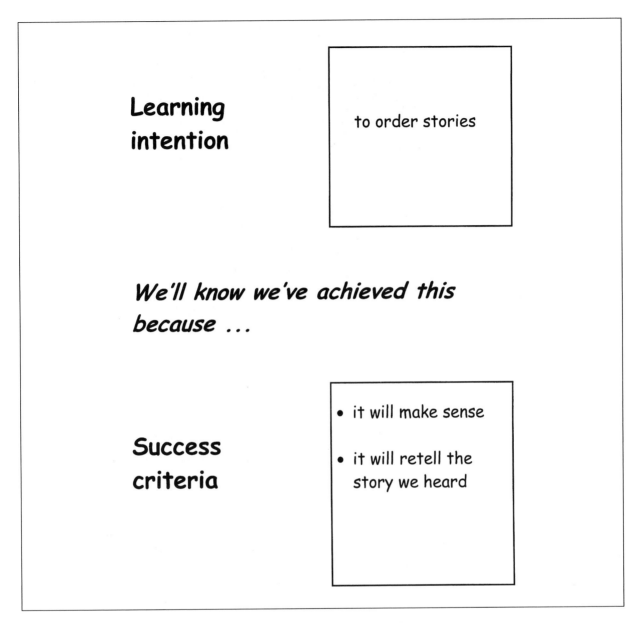

**Learning intention**

to order stories

**We'll know we've achieved this because ...**

**Success criteria**

- it will make sense

- it will retell the story we heard

*Fig. 2.3 The learning intention and success criteria on a flipchart page*

In this instance, teachers usually write the learning intention only and explain to the children that for each group she will be looking for different things. Each group is told verbally, when the teacher sets them off on their work. If time permits, some teachers write the success criteria for each group on a sheet of paper and place this on the group's table, as in the photograph on page 30.

*Fig. 2.4 Success criteria for a group*

**2** **There might be one learning intention for several lessons, with different success criteria as the work progresses.**
Explain this to the children at the first lesson.

**3** **There might be several learning intentions because the original learning intention has had to be broken down, to accommodate different abilities.**
Write up the broad learning intention (e.g. Ordering to at least 1000), explaining that the separate tasks are all different aspects of this (e.g. some have ordering to 100 and some to 10,000).

**4** **There might be several unrelated learning intentions across the class (especially in a Reception class) where completely different activities sometimes take place at once.**

If the children rotate around the groups, it is easier to have four different learning intention and success criteria displays, colour-coded so each group knows which is theirs. To avoid confusion with younger children organised in this way, some teachers just write up the learning intentions, leaving the success criteria as an oral statement only.

Ultimately, it is up to teachers to use their common sense when using learning intention and success criteria boards or charts, remembering, of course, that the visual display is probably the most important aspect of sharing learning intentions.

# Questions teachers often ask

### 1 Is it still appropriate to display the learning intentions and success criteria for children who can't read it?

Yes, most definitely. Imagine you are learning a new language and the teacher is speaking that language throughout the lesson, so most of your understanding is derived from the spoken word. Imagine the teacher writes one of the words she says on a flip chart and points to it, again saying the word. The word stays on display for the whole lesson. What are you most likely to remember about the lesson, even if you could not actually 'read' the word? Children remember words made visually obvious in this way, even though they cannot 'read' them.

### 2 Is it a good idea to write up the learning intention and success criteria in advance of the lesson?

Write the learning intention, but not the success criteria. Children need to be invited, whenever possible, to create the success criteria with you. Also, writing it in advance can lead to a situation where the teacher tries to explain to the class the words she has written. Wait until the phrasing used in the classroom reveals some understanding, then write those words in the success criteria speech bubble. Teachers often find it useful to write the learning intentions and success criteria in their short-term plans, so they are 'tuned in'.

*3*  **Should the success criteria be a summary of the activity?**
No – it should be what you are going to judge the children on at the end of the task. If the task involved sticking and gluing, cutting and ordering, the children need to know what will be the prime focus. The activity instructions have made clear what has to be done – the *How will we know we've done this?* makes clear what is most important in concrete, quantified terms.

*4*  **How can I write up every learning intention for a Literacy Hour?**
You only need to display learning intentions for the main part of the lesson, where children are asked to go off and do some work on their own which they will be judged on. Text-level work, say, is best dealt with by explaining learning intentions verbally, as part of the class discussion or direct teaching. However, if there are only two learning intentions overall, for instance, the teacher might decide it is worth writing both up.

*5*  **What about 'closed' learning intentions?**
Many of the Numeracy and Literacy learning intentions are 'closed'. Where this happens, the activity is likely to be closed and the success criteria tend to look very like the learning intention. For example:

**Activity:** putting the correct spelling of *their, they're* or *there* into given sentences.

**Learning intention:** It will help you learn to use the correct spelling of *their, they're* and *there*.

**Success criteria:** You'll have used the sense of the sentence to choose the correct spelling of *their, they're* or *there*.

*6*  **Does that mean more 'open' learning intentions are more tricky?**
Yes, although very open learning intentions can lead to very open success criteria. For example, finding out the effect of exercise on the heart is likely to lead to a success criterion which says, for example, you have found out and can explain, by the end of your experiment, what happens to the heart rate when we exercise.

**7  Does it matter if I make the activity do more than the learning intention requires?**

No. It is vital that we remember that the learning intentions of the National Curriculum, and Literacy and Numeracy Strategies are the *minimum* requirement. Once we are sure that the activity planned will cover that requirement, we should do whatever we feel is necessary to make the activity more interesting and more far-reaching.

For example, if we restrict the learning intention of locating towns on a map to just that, the task will be closed, relatively dull and undemanding for many children. If, however, we extend the task to then find the shortest route from one town to another, or to then try to find out how the towns compare in population, we involve the children in higher-order skills. This means that we have changed the learning intention, but the minimum requirement is still intact. Such changes would occur at the short-term stage, when teachers know their children and how the topic is developing, so are clearer about what is possible.

What does matter is that the activity matches the learning intention. In order to save time, it can be tempting to bend the learning intention to match the activity you want to do. This is only acceptable if the original learning intention will be covered within that activity. Problems arise if aspects of learning intentions are left out, especially process elements like 'using and applying'.

**8  How do I know if children understand the learning intention and success criteria?**

A common approach is to ask children to indicate, through signals, the level of their understanding. For instance, a thumbs-up signal for 'understand', and a thumbs sideways signal for 'not sure'. Make it clear to children that it is *your* fault if even one child is unsure, and rephrase the explanation. This has very positive effects on children in that they see misunderstanding as the teacher's responsibility rather than their lack of ability: a noticeable rise in self-esteem occurs.

**9  Won't Year 6 children get bored with characters?**

Many children still seem to like it, but there are also many cases where the teacher uses acronyms without the character(s). In any case, do not place too much emphasis on the characters.

*10*    **Should children write the learning intention in their books?**

Only when they are fluent writers and this would take about a minute of their time. Too often children are asked to copy out learning intentions on to their work as the title, which can take up to ten minutes. This is clearly a waste of children's time, even though, in an ideal world, learning intentions on all work would be useful. Teachers can write learning intentions on worksheets which are then to be photocopied, but attempting to put learning intentions on all work is impossible for younger children without losing valuable teaching and learning time. If learning intentions are clearly written in short-term plans for every lesson (see Chapter 1), children's work can always be cross-referenced to plans in order to identify the learning intention, if need be.

# The impact of sharing learning intentions

## *The impact on children*

- Children are more focused. Teachers' definition of *focused* is that children:
  - have more staying power;
  - talk about the learning intention;
  - are excited by it;
  - are able to recognise their achievement;
  - are pleased with the outcomes of their endeavours, even if they need more help;
  - change their emphasis from completion of the task to achievement of the learning intention;
  - work for themselves rather than for the teacher;
  - produce work which relates to the learning intention rather than a 'rag bag';
  - say *'What are we going to learn?'* rather than *'What are we going to do?'*.

- Children demand the learning intention if it is forgotten, as they soon realise how important it is to their understanding of the task.

- Teachers have been amazed at how easily Reception children have been able to create the success criteria.

- Children are more likely to express their learning needs (e.g. *'I would like to work on my own in order to learn this', 'I would find a number line easier'*, etc.) as it gives them permission to question what is being done to them.

- A learning culture develops in the school, as children start to use the language of the learning intentions rather than the language of the activities.

- The quality of the work improves: in the amount done, in the adherence to the learning intention and success criteria of the task, and in children's ability to produce their best.

- Children of below average and average ability are noticeably more focused.

- Some teachers have reported that this strategy has an especially noticeable impact on low-achieving boys. The belief is that the 'aside' motivates them, helping these children know the 'real life' reason and context for their learning in school.

- Children's behaviour improves as their task focus increases.

- Children persevere for longer at a task.

- Children have greater ownership of the lesson, as responsibility for the learning is shifted from the teacher to the child.

- Children are put into an automatically self-evaluative position.

- Children are more enthusiastic about learning.

- Stating learning intentions makes a plenary or subsequent reflection against the learning intention a necessity.

## The impact on teachers

- It forces the teacher to be more focused on the learning intention than the activity.

- It sharpens the teacher's understanding of the learning intention.

■ Teacher expectations rise.

■ It makes teachers focus naturally on quality rather than getting everything done.

■ Teachers are more critical of activities, focusing on whether they would enable children to meet the learning intention and whether the success criteria would be clear.

■ Stating the learning intention reinforces the relevant vocabulary.

■ Stating the 'aside' – why this is important to learn at all – encourages children to make links with other lessons (e.g. reasons for learning about fractions helped a class understand decimals more easily the next day).

■ Stating learning intentions makes a plenary or subsequent reflection against the learning intention a necessity.

Where one teacher used A4 paper on the whiteboard, sticking them onto the learning intention and success criteria bubbles, tearing them off each time to fall on the floor after each lesson, children became interested in the pile of learning intentions and how much they had learnt at the end of the day. The teacher capitalised on this interest by coordinating a class discussion at the end of the day about what had been learnt throughout the day. She then started to display a timetable for the week's learning intentions (not the activities) at the request of the children, finding that their first interest on Monday was *'What will we be learning this week?'* Another teacher began a list on the classroom wall of all the learning intentions, which were added to each week, again stimulating great interest by children, parents and other adults. We should not be surprised that, once given the responsibility for and a stake in their own learning, children should want to know in advance what they will be learning.

## *Wider implications and effects*

■ Parents start expressing an interest in learning intentions, and might even ask for explanations!

■ The use of learning intentions and success criteria has given increased opportunities for links with parents in some schools, where parents were encouraged to carry on talking about these at home, rather than focusing on spellings, for instance.

■ If it is a whole-school approach, monitoring of lessons is more likely to focus on whether children knew the learning intention and whether that was the focus of lessons.

■ Many schools have capitalised on the potential of the language of learning intentions and success criteria (*'We are learning to'* and *'How will you know you've done that?'*) for situations beyond the classroom, for instance for helpers controlling behaviour on the playground.

### INSET ideas

1.  Introduce the ideas to the teachers, discussing how the posters of '*We are learning to...*' and success criteria will be organised.

2.  Hold a staff meeting in which teachers bring along short-term plans. In pairs they choose a learning intention, and its activity, and create a childspeak learning intention, success criteria and 'aside' (the reason for doing this). Get each pair to read out the original learning intention, then the learning intention, success criteria and 'aside' and get all staff to rework these until all are happy. After hearing all attempts, and analysing and modifying them, teachers feel more confident about sharing learning intentions in the classroom. However, this meeting often throws up problems, with learning intentions in short-term plans being too broad or not matching activities. It is often the case that you do not know what can be improved in planning until you try to create childspeak learning intentions and especially success criteria. Teachers need to trial the sharing of learning intentions in this way in order to improve their skills.

3.  Make sure every teacher is given the pictures, posters or whiteboards. Some headteachers have reported that teachers often don't get round to creating the posters themselves so the strategy is not applied evenly throughout the school.

4.  Teachers should begin by sharing for one subject only, then two, then all other subjects.

5.   After about half a term, hold a feedback meeting where every teacher gives short, timed feedback about the impact of sharing learning intentions in this way, including successes, problems and strategies to overcome difficulties. The meeting will strengthen the practice for all teachers.

6.   Make the strategies high profile in the school, by having *We are learning to...* and *How will we know you've done that?* in assembly and by mentioning them in sharing assemblies. Children and teachers then see that this is a whole-school approach with a shared language.

# 3 Pupil self-evaluation

Many studies show significant progress made by children who have been trained to be self-evaluative. *Assessment for Learning: Beyond the Black Box* (Assessment Reform Group, 1999) outlines some of the key issues:

> *Current thinking about learning acknowledges that learners must ultimately be responsible for their learning since no one else can do it for them. Thus assessment for learning must involve pupils, so as to provide them with information about how well they are doing and guide their subsequent efforts. Much of this information will come as feedback from the teacher, but some will be through their direct involvement in assessing their own work. The awareness of learning and ability of learners to direct it for themselves is of increasing importance in the context of encouraging lifelong learning.*

Sadler (1989) described the importance of enabling children to be self-evaluative:

> *Part of the teacher's responsibility is, surely, to download that evaluative knowledge so that students eventually become independent of the teacher and intelligently engage in and monitor their own development. If anything, the guild knowledge of teachers should consist less in knowing how to evaluate student work and more in **knowing ways to download evaluative knowledge to students.***
>
> (Sadler, 1989)

Once learning intentions are established and shared with children, the self-evaluation during and especially at the end of the lesson becomes a necessity. A major part of the plenary of a lesson should be children's reflective comments about their learning, followed by teacher summary, unravelling misconceptions and providing links with future learning. HMI reports indicate that Literacy and Numeracy plenaries are often focused mainly around children sharing their work, which is in many ways a waste of opportunity for self-evaluative thinking.

Research shows that if self-evaluation is linked with the learning intentions of a task, children's progress, persistence and self-esteem is improved (Black and Wiliam, 1998). Training needs include helping children to see how to answer a self-evaluative question, teaching them how to think and getting into the habit of linking questions with the learning intention.

# Training children to be self-evaluative during plenaries

*1*    As with sharing learning intentions, explain to the class the purpose of self-evaluation sessions (part of plenary).

*2*    Reiterate the learning intention during the course of a lesson.

*3*    Capitalise on the power of the visual image by displaying a range of self-evaluative questions for ends of lessons.

**The poster opposite shows possible self-evaluative questions**
(… represents the learning intention each time – it is easy to forget to link the question with the learning intention.)

*4*    To begin with, spend from one to three weeks, at ends of lessons, simply **modelling** the possible answers children might have to the self-evaluative questions (*'I think some of you might say you're most pleased with…'* etc.), and asking them not to answer the questions yet, to stop brighter children hijacking the session. This shows children *(a)* how to answer a self-evaluation question and *(b)* that all children

# Self evaluation:

## thinking about what happens when we are learning

*(Choose one or two and add the words of the learning intention)*

- **What really made you think/did you find difficult while you were learning to** ... ?

- **What helped you** (e.g. a friend, the teacher, new equipment, a book, your own thinking) **when something got tricky about learning to** ... ?

- **What do you need more help with about learning to** ... ?

- **What are you most pleased with about learning to** ... ?

- **What have you learnt that is new about** ... (quote learning intention)?

- **How would you change this activity for another group/class who were learning to** ... ?

experience difficulties regardless of their apparent ability. Children naturally assume that more able children never find anything difficult, but this process makes explicit that all learners experience the same aspects, at their level. It is in confronting the second question in the poster that we change the 'fear of failure' culture to a 'difficulty means learning' culture.

5    After the training period of modelling answers, choose one question for ends of lessons, and link it explicitly with the learning intention (e.g. *'What are you most pleased with about understanding pushes and pulls?'*)

6    Allow a short period (15–30 seconds) of **thinking time** after giving children a self-evaluative question (heads down, eyes down, don't move – eye contact and body movements distract you and others from thinking).

7    Use a variety of approaches for different days, after modelling possible answers: whole-class responses, paired responses, group responses. (Between 2 and 10 minutes, depending on the type of lesson and what is manageable.)

8    Avoid getting children to *write* their self-evaluations, as their thinking will be reduced to what is easy to write.

## Fear of failure

A critical element of encouraging self-evaluative thinking is how the teacher deals with situations where children find their work difficult or are 'stuck'. The language used by the teacher in lessons is highly influential in building the culture of the classroom. The following examples of how to deal with these situations have resulted in noticeable 'unlocking' of children's thinking and a rise in their self-esteem:

❝ *I'm really pleased you've noticed you are stuck. I need to find out what you need and then you will be able to learn something new.* ❞

❝ *Well done – if it's making you think, you are learning! Let's find out how you can be helped with that learning.* ❞

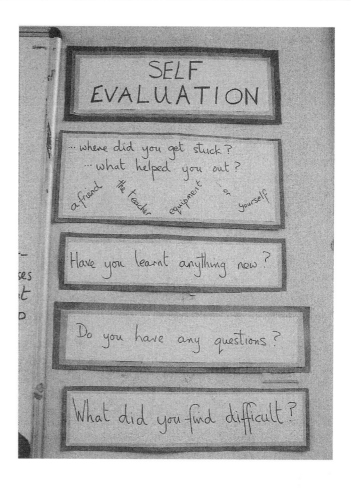

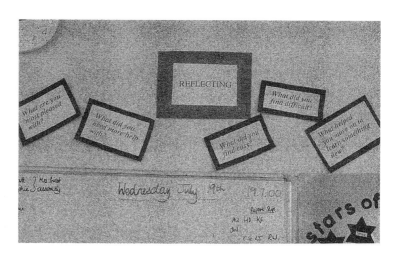

*Fig. 3.1 Examples of self-evaluation questions in the classroom*

> ❝ *It's great that you are finding that tricky – it means you are learning! See if you can tell me what it is that I need to help you with, so that you will be able to learn something new.* ❞

> ❝ *I'm a bit worried that you're finding this too easy. I'm pleased with what you've done so far, but unless this makes you think more you're probably not going to be learning something new. Let's talk together about how we can make this more challenging for you.* ❞

This approach eliminates the culture of striving for work to be easy. It also stops children complaining of copying, because looking at how someone else has done something is seen as an important learning cue. Notice each time that the difficulty is linked with new learning.

# The impact of pupil self-evaluation as part of the plenary

## The impact on children

■ The greatest impact on children is an overall rise in their **self-esteem**. This is a well-researched result of pupil self-evaluation. Teachers have been particularly excited by the evidence of this, saying that children are:
  - able to say where they need help without any sense of failure;
  - working towards being in control of their own learning;
  - beginning to set their own targets and goals (e.g. *'I found this difficult because I don't know my tables – I need to learn them'*);
  - now able to speak about their learning when they would not have done before;
  - aware of what they have learnt and feel confident that they can talk about it;
  - more inclined to talk about their own learning in general (e.g. *'I've learnt if I keep trying I get there in the end'*).

■ Children seem to have been liberated by the language used by teachers that their difficulties are good, because the difficulty signals what needs to happen to enable them to learn. A typical quote from children is *'It's OK if you don't know something – it helps Miss to know what she needs to do next.'* One child was reported as having very little confidence in writing. After self-evaluation sessions he said, reiterating the teacher's words, *'I'm pleased I found it hard because now I know what to do next.'* He repeated this statement to the teacher the next day, and from that day started to write. Children also seem relieved to hear that looking at someone else's work is an important learning prompt. Other quotes include:

*'I never thought that group found maths hard.'*
*'When it is difficult for us, that is when we are learning.'*
*'I've learnt that sometimes you need to slow down and then you get your work right.'*

■ Children also enjoy finding that other children often have exactly the same thoughts, sharing similar problems or successes during self-evaluation sessions.

■ Teachers often mention children's enthusiasm for self-evaluation sessions. Children enjoy picking the self-evaluation question themselves at times, and often want to carry on through lunchtime. One teacher was astonished that the boys in her class wanted to miss football in order to carry on with self-evaluation!

■ Children's mathematics can improve as a result of the self-evaluation, because the questions focus on *how* the maths had been done rather than on *what* had been done.

Teachers often say, as can be gleaned from the case studies overleaf, that they learn more from the self-evaluation session about future planning than through any other process. Although self-evaluation develops children's awareness of their learning needs, it also opens doors for teachers into children's minds.

## Case Study 1

One teacher kept track of certain children's self-evaluation comments for the course she was attending. These children were deliberately chosen because they had low self-esteem, generally underachieved and found it difficult to articulate.

**Tuesday: Learning intention (L.I.) *To evaluate texts for effective and interesting descriptions.***

Daniel said, *'I found this difficult but people reading out their ideas helped me move on.'*

**Wednesday: L.I. *To identify linking connectives.***

In answer to what helped you get out of a difficulty, Shane said, *'I was stuck and James helped me on the end bit.'*

**L.I. *To add and subtract pairs of two-digit numbers mentally.***

Shane said, *'I found it difficult to break the numbers down (partitioning) and Mrs Wright helped me understand.'*

The teacher did more of this in the next mental session.

James said, *'What I found helpful was when Daniel did his method on the board – it showed me what to do.'*

Katy said, *'What I realised is that I do that method in my head.'*

**Thursday: L.I. *To identify features of persuasive texts.***

Nicola said, *'They made it easy (in the text) by numbering the points of view.'*

**L.I. *To add and subtract using a calculator.***

Daniel said, *'What I found difficult is the standard written method and I realised I could use jottings – it helped me more.'*

The teacher described all these comments as 'a breakthrough for these children'.

## *The impact on teachers*

■ Teachers report increased insight into children's learning needs, including when work is too easy for them – something which children often keep to themselves without the honesty of self-evaluation sessions. One teacher's response reveals new understanding: *'It helps you to value pupils – to know how they're thinking – to know what it feels like to be them. I used to feel that I was doing lessons to*

## Case Study 2

Another teacher planned a Year 6 lesson as follows:

**Learning intention:** *To be able to name and design a mini project based on the theme 'World issues'.*

**How will I know?:** What I'm looking for is to see how you plan and organise your project and tell us about it through a two-minute speech.

**Aside:** We're doing this so that you can become more responsible and involved in the project we'll be doing next term.

After a class brainstorm, the children worked at the task.

The self-evaluation question was *'Have you learnt anything new about designing a project on world issues?'*

The teacher first modelled some possible answers:

*'I think some of you might say you have learnt how to organise a project from beginning to end.'*

*'I think some of you might say you've learnt that two minutes is a long time, especially if you haven't planned well.'*

*'I think some of you might say you've learnt that a brainstorm is not enough in organising and planning a project.'*

Children's responses included:

*'Planning is more important than starting straight away writing facts.'*

*'I learnt to just jot down some pointers to help me in my plan.'*

*'I've learnt that I need to do more research before I even plan.'*

*'I've learnt that it's not so easy to come up with ideas. You need to be organised – what you need to do first, then second and so on.'*

get through the curriculum, whereas now I'm constantly reminded that I'm there to get them to learn – it reinforces your responsibility as a teacher.'

■ The modelling stage is seen as crucial, before questions are opened up for the whole class or paired responses. Teachers often report on the nodding or shaking of heads while they are suggesting children's possible thoughts, and on less able children using the suggested responses as future strategies. The 'thinking time' is enjoyed by children, with younger ones seeing it as a special time, which they seem surprisingly excited about!

■ In the early stages, in some classes, it takes time for children to respond to the questions, but this is usually a transient period. As one teacher said, *'I think that once you come to the point where things become embedded in what you do, things become manageable. It's the time when you are moving from one set of processes to another where inevitably you are not going to be able to do it well overnight. It's something that you gradually introduce and get better at.'*

■ After a few months, the poster of questions has less importance, because the questions become embedded in everyone's consciousness, and new ones are thought of.

■ One teacher of older children asked them to write *'This was too easy'*, *'I could do this'* or *'I need help with this'* at the end of their work. She found this added to the verbal self-evaluation and enabled her to learn even more about their perceptions of their learning.

■ In terms of finding the time, this is already catered for in Literacy and Numeracy Hours through the plenary. For other lessons, the same time or shorter bursts can be used, according to teachers' planning. One teacher said, in response to questions from other teachers in her school about time to do self-evaluation: *'Self-evaluation is part of learning, so finding time is not an issue – it's part of the lesson, not an extra thing.'*

■ Teachers found their plenary was more focused and relevant, and saved time by writing 'Self-evaluation poster' in their plans for plenary sessions.

The link with and feedback into planning shows how valuable pupil self-evaluation is as an assessment tool, with assessment information very clearly being used to inform future planning. However, as demonstrated, it is important that the essence of the session is about thinking, articulating, making contact and giving positive body language, for both teacher and children, based on the original focus of the explicit sharing of learning intentions.

The enthusiasm of the children should be no surprise, considering the clear increase in their self-esteem. The refocus on **difficulty**, or where something **'makes you think'**, is of particular importance in helping children see learning as a continuum, with the teacher as one source of getting their learning *right*. With more time, children become more able to identify and solve their own learning needs.

**INSET ideas**

1.  At a staff meeting, show teachers the research quotations about the impact and importance of self-evaluation. Go through the poster of questions, highlighting the key points and the role of modelling. Emphasise the importance of changing the language of difficulties and getting stuck. Ask teachers to tell the children about this, display the poster and begin the modelling stage. After two weeks remind everyone to go on to opening up the discussions.

2.  Have a feedback meeting after about six weeks, asking each teacher to feed back successes, problems, and impact on children and teacher. Ask teachers in advance to jot down anything children say, which would be useful to share with others at this feedback meeting. During the meeting, focus on the impact on children and how the teacher used the information from self-evaluation when it threw up learning needs which were previously invisible.

3.  Talk about self-evaluation around the school – in assemblies and so on – to raise its profile.

4.  Ensure that classroom observations include self-evaluation as one of the monitoring criteria, regardless of the subject involved.

# 4 Feedback

This chapter deals with two aspects of feedback: oral and written, including marking. It focuses mainly on feedback from teacher to child, but this develops to include children's feedback to each other. Pupils' self-evaluation, dealt with in the previous chapter, involves a great deal of pupil feedback to the teacher.

## Oral feedback when the class is at work

Various research studies have concluded that feedback is most useful when it focuses on the **learning intention** of the task, rather than other features of the work. However, research also shows that most teachers give feedback to children about four other features of their work before, or even instead of, the learning intention of the task:

- presentation (handwriting/neatness);
- surface features of writing (full stops, capital letters and especially spelling);
- quantity;
- effort.

It is easy to see why this happens: those aspects are most noticeable in children's work at first sight. They are also relatively straightforward to deal with. Ironically, these are the very things teachers accuse parents of focusing on at parents' evenings.

### What can happen...

The children have been asked to cut out, order and then glue muddled-up pictures of a story onto a piece of paper.

Learning intentions and success criteria are displayed prominently as follows:

> **We Are Learning To:** Order stories.
>
> **How will we know we've done this?:** The pictures will be in the same order as the story we read.

■ As the children start to work, the teacher notices that one child already has glue all over his trousers. She goes to the child and speaks to him, getting him to go quickly to the washroom to clean up. The rest of the group starts to fuss about glue. One child rushes to get a cloth as she notices glue on her table and the whole class starts to chat about glue or anything else....

■ The teacher notices a child having difficulty cutting out and goes over to help her hold the scissors correctly, talking about how much better she is getting at this. One child tells the teacher that she's been able to cut out properly for a year now. Some children, having roughly cut out two of their pictures are now going back to them and cutting them out more neatly, because they don't want the teacher to criticise their cutting. They had not cut out neatly in the first place because they thought the emphasis was on ordering....

■ The teacher passes a child who has, at last, written her name on the paper with a capital letter at the beginning of her name. She praises the child enthusiastically. Some of the children now cross out their names on their sheets, because they realise they had also forgotten to do this....

■ The teacher congratulates one child who is working industriously, saying how pleased she is to see her working so hard. The children sit up straighter to get some praise themselves....

So far, the class knows that the learning intention and success criteria are a lie. The teacher has made clear by her words that what she is looking for is not the ordering, but presentation, surface features, effort and cutting skills.

# An alternative approach...

The following scenario describes a strategy for giving feedback focused around the same learning intention:

■ As the children start to work, the teacher notices that one child already has glue all over his trousers. She goes to the child and first says something about the learning intention: *'Well done, I can see you've got the first picture in place. Now what happened next in the story, after the Little Red Hen had dug the ground?'* Some of the children quietly call out *'planted the seeds'* and continue with their ordering. The teacher then whispers to the child, *'You've got glue on your trousers. Go and clean up quickly.'*

■ The teacher notices a child having difficulty cutting out. She moves to her and congratulates her on cutting out all the pictures first: *'That's a very good strategy. You have cut out all the pictures first so that you can shuffle them around and change your mind.'* Some of the children are now peeling off their stuck-down pictures, because they agree that it is a very good strategy. The teacher then whispers to the child about holding the scissors.

So far, the class knows that the learning intention and success criteria are the truth. The teacher has made clear by her words that what she is looking for is *ordering*.

This technique has been received very powerfully by teachers, who realise how often they have fallen into the trap of focusing on other features and distracting the class from the prime focus of their learning. One teacher said:

❛ *I recognised things in myself like commenting about the handwriting and spelling, when I should be commenting on the learning intention. It's been a real revelation to me. I'm aware of it all the time now and when I hear myself starting to say "You've left a capital letter out there", I stop really quickly now and go back to talking about the learning intention.* ❜

It takes a while to get into the habit, but the strategy is simple: hold on to the thought about the secondary feature and make sure that something about the learning intention is mentioned *first*, then mention the glue or handwriting, if it is necessary, in a whisper. The class will retain their focus on the learning intention, which will be apparent in their improved work.

# Marking

Research shows that marking is often directly responsible for *regression* in many pupils, and that traditional practice tends to demoralise and overwhelm pupils, with children often making no sense of it. Bearing in mind the urgent need to improve children's writing, in particular, it is timely to begin to reconsider current beliefs and practices in marking.

## The problems

### Stuck in a rut

One of the problems about marking is that teachers are often embedded in a way of working which is hard to break. Teachers have typically marked children's work by automatically correcting spelling errors and other surface features, acting as a copy editor in a publishing firm, then providing comments at the end. The information is too much for children to process. Teachers often feel that they are marking for an inspector or for parents, when the main purpose of the marking feedback should be to give information to *children* about how well they did against the learning intention.

### Giving children too many criteria at the beginning of a task

After sharing learning intentions and making sure children know what to do, it is often the case that the children are then given up to six more learning intentions to pay attention to (e.g. *'What I'm looking for in this letter to the Prime Minister is that you have used persuasive language. Oh, and don't forget your best handwriting, correct spellings, capital letters and full-stops, grammar, punctuation and paragraphs.'*) Children now have seven criteria to deal with in perhaps 20 or 30 minutes.

Research shows that, in these circumstances, children pay most attention to what the teacher makes clear, by her actions, means the most to her. So a teacher who continually mentions handwriting will have beautiful handwriting in her class, but the children will be producing less work than they could. Always focusing on handwriting slows children down.

The same is true for spelling. Research shows that children can only spell correctly words that they *know* how to spell, so it is of little use to tell them to make sure their spellings are correct. Children learn to spell by the specific teaching of spelling (word- and sentence-level work), by looking at patterns and doing work where a spelling rule is the learning intention, and also by reading. Asking children to check spellings continuously only leads to spelling becoming too dominant in the writing process. Children worry disproportionately about their spelling and get out of their seats to look up words, often talking to other children on the way. They have by then often lost the thread of their sentence. Ironically, copying out the correct spelling in their work from the word book does not then help them to spell that word correctly the next time they want to use it. It has wasted their time. Worrying about spelling also stops children trying adventurous words and can lead to misspelt words being 'corrected' by them to an alternative misspelt word, or worse, a correct spelling can be 'corrected' by the child so that it is then misspelt.

Expecting children to apply all the criteria they have ever been taught for every piece of writing means that we are treating every piece of writing *as a test*. It is only in test situations that we ask children to apply all their learnt skills. Imagine making every mathematics lesson a maths test! We know that children's maths progress would be very slow, as has been evident in children's writing. In maths we introduce one skill at a time, teach children to develop that skill, later make sure they apply it and, at regular intervals, test it. We need to do the same with writing, giving children feedback about the learning intention only, ignoring spellings and other features, unless that is the learning intention. On a regular basis we need to ask children to apply all they know about writing in a test essay. Many schools have extended writing lessons every week where children operate in these conditions. Literacy advisors have pointed out that this is not a good idea, because it simply gives children time to practise more of their mistakes, so once every four weeks or half a term would seem more appropriate. In the meantime, we need to be focusing on specific aspects of writing in order to help children develop their skills.

## Giving too much feedback at the end

Having given many criteria at the beginning of the task, we often then give children too much information through marking, which is overwhelming and difficult for children to take in. They are often demoralised by it, especially if there are many spelling errors pointed out when the child's writing was in fact very good.

One of the most important research findings is that grading every piece of work is counterproductive. This mainly applies to secondary schools of course, but there are parallels in primary schools. Grades freeze children into 'ego-related mode' rather than 'task-related mode'. Anyone who gets B or above is likely to feel complacent and anyone with B minus or below tends to feel demoralised. Grades beg instant comparisons with classmates, again leading to complacency or demoralisation. Children ignore marking *comments* when a grade or symbol is present, because that becomes the most important measure of their ability and achievement. Instead, research shows that children should be given information about where they achieved success against the learning intention and where they could improve against the learning intention – both at the same time. For instance, given a learning intention of using effective adjectives, we might say *'These are the three best adjectives you used and this one needs improving.'* Pointing out the success of the adjectives, then stating that the spelling could be improved, does not fit this formula. Every now and again children do need to know where their work lies in comparison with a standard – but not for every piece of work.

Although grades are rarely used in primary schools, stickers often are. These can act in the same way as a grade, distracting children from other feedback. External rewards are dealt with in detail in Chapter 8.

# *Distance marking*

Distance marking – marking away from the children, because there is simply no alternative – takes up much of teachers' lives. Much of my specific research has focused on ways to make distance marking more manageable for teachers and more meaningful and accessible for children. Research about distance marking shows that children need to be able to *read* the teacher's comments and *understand* them. Understanding is often absent, and only the most confident and able children ask teachers to explain marking comments to them. Most children do not ask because they do not want to lose face by making the teacher think they do not understand what she has written.

Children also need to be given set lesson time to read marking comments, and then a short period of time to make a small, focused improvement based on the comments. Without the feedback information being used by the child, the improvement suggestion is unlikely to be carried over to future work in different contexts. For instance, writing *'You could say more about the prince'* will only be worthwhile if the child is then asked to use this prompt to write another sentence about the prince, thus improving the work against the learning intention.

Sadler (1989), in his paper about formative assessment, established three conditions for effective feedback to take place: the child must first know the **purpose** of the task, then how far they achieved this, and finally how to move closer towards the desired goal, or how to **'close the gap'** between what they have done and what they could do.

It is often the case that, instead of giving specific, concrete strategies to help children move from what they have achieved to what we want them to achieve, teachers instead simply reiterate the desired goal. For example, *'You need to give a better description here'* merely reiterates the learning goal of 'write a descriptive story opening'. Better advice would be that which focuses on how to improve the description (e.g. *'What was the prince wearing?'*, *'Could you describe just the prince's face?'*).

Time management is, of course, of prime concern in getting children to read then act on marking – but a personal anecdote perhaps emphasises the importance for learning:

*I sing in a choir. Some time ago, we stumbled over two bars and the conductor stopped us and sang the two bars to us. We listened carefully. He then said 'OK? Everyone turn to page 167.' The next time we arrived at the passage we stumbled again. Our conductor was cross, accusing us of not listening and yet again sang it to us. It was not unusual for this to happen three or four times, with the same passage, before a concert.*

*What he should have done, of course, after singing it to us, was to have asked us to sing it back to him. He would have learnt two things from this: (a) whether we now knew the passage, and (b) if we hadn't, where we were going wrong. So why doesn't he do this? Because he feels that he doesn't have time. Every week he places an A4 sheet on his stand of all the numbers we need to get through. He then spends the entire evening looking between his list and the clock. His measure of success is that he has reached the end of his list. If he only had the courage to leave one or two numbers out, over time, we would know the piece better.*

There are some powerful parallels here with lessons today, with teachers often feeling they are on a conveyor belt, aiming to cover the curriculum. If learning is our prime concern, then we cannot afford *not* to give children time to read and act on our feedback. It is one of the most significant aspects of learning. Some strategies for finding time and making this happen are given in the following pages.

## A practical strategy for 'closing the gap' in marking

The research shows that we need to be giving feedback about the learning intention: indicating success and improvement needs. Marking can be more accessible for children if we introduce codes to show these elements, as follows:

*1*  **Highlight (with a highlighter pen) three places where the child has written the best aspects against the learning intention and indicate with an arrow/asterisk where some improvement can be made.**
In *Targeting Assessment in the Primary Classroom* (Clarke, 1998), this strategy was in its early stages. The initial findings were that children loved the highlights, but hated the arrows! Their reasons were that they did not know *how* to make the improvement.

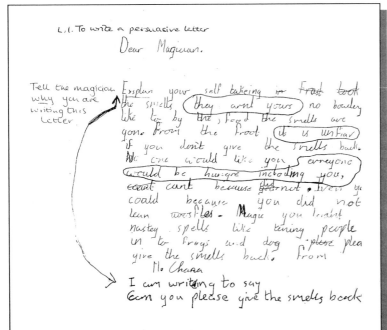

L.I. To write a persuasive letter

Dear Magician.

Tell the magician why you are writing this letter.

Explain your self takeing the smells (they arnt yours) no border like to by the food the smells are gone from the froot (it is unfair) if you dont give the smells back. No one would like you (everyone would be hungre including you, eeast cant because for not even you coald because you did not learn worst les. Mague you learnt nastey spells like tuning people in to frogs and dog please plea give the smells back. from M. Chaea

I am writing to say Can you please give the smells back

*Fig. 4.1 The Magician who stole all the smells: persuasive letter*

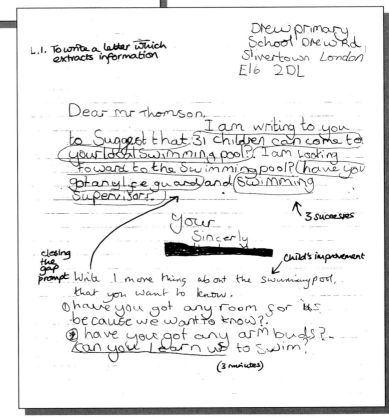

L.I. To write a letter which extracts information

Drew Primary School Drew Rd, Silvertown London E16 2DL

Dear mr Thomson,
I am writing to you to Suggest that 31 children can come to your local swimming pool. I am looking foward to the swimming pool? have you got any life guard and swimming Supervisors.

↑ 3 successes

Your Sincerly ▬▬▬▬

closing the gap prompt

child's improvement

Write 1 more thing about the swimming pool, that you want to know.
① have you got any room for us because we want to know?
② have you got any arm buds? Can you learn us to swim?

(3 minutes)

*Fig. 4.2 Learning intention: Writing a letter to extract information*

2 **The next stage of trialling was for the teacher to extend the arrow to the nearest white space and write a 'closing the gap' prompt for the child, to help them to close the gap and be able to make a small improvement.**
This was the start of a great deal of interest by teachers, because now subsequent alterations made by children showed real improvement. The illustrations show examples of this strategy in action, with the child's subsequent improvement at the end. In Figure 4.1, the highlights indicate best persuasive language. The teacher has chosen to place the arrow at the beginning, asking the child to tell the magician why she is writing, a basic good start to a persuasive letter. Figure 4.4 shows the three best similes, in the teacher's opinion, and an arrow by the final line, with a 'closing the gap' prompt which focuses the child specifically on the way the cat is staring. The child's subsequent improvement makes a marked difference to the end of the poem.

Over time, it has been possible to categorise the different types of 'closing the gap' comments teachers have written, which has, in turn, given teachers more support in finding the right words with which to effectively 'close the gap' for each child.

## 'Closing the gap' prompt categories

A practical example helps to illustrate the different types of responses:

**Learning Intention:** To effectively introduce a character at the start of a story.

**Activity:** The children have to choose someone they know, who the class will not know, to describe.

**We are learning to:** *Write about people's characters effectively in our stories.*

**How will we know we've done this?** (created with the class): *We will have said something about their appearance, their likes and dislikes (including hobbies), their general personality, their attitude to others, anything else.*

**Aside:** *This is important because it helps the reader to really feel they know the person, rather than just knowing what they look like.*

After highlighting three success phrases (or perhaps just one for younger children), imagine the teacher has placed the arrow at the line written by the child: *'This person is a good friend.'* The following 'closing the gap' prompts are possible:

### 1    A reminder prompt

Most suitable for brighter children, this simply reminds the child of what could be improved:

> *Say more about how you feel about*
> *this person*

Interestingly, many teachers write this kind of prompt for all children. Most children need more support than a reminder prompt.

### 2    A scaffolded prompt

Most suitable for children who need more structure than a simple reminder, this prompt provides some support.

| | |
|---|---|
| *Can you describe how this person is 'a good friend'?* | *A question* |

**or**

| | |
|---|---|
| *Describe something that happened which showed you they were a good friend* | *A directive* |

**or**

| | |
|---|---|
| *He showed me he was a good friend when.......... (finish this sentence)* | *An unfinished sentence* |

### 3    An example prompt

Extremely successful with all children, but especially with average or below average children, this prompt gives the child a choice of actual words or phrases.

| | |
|---|---|
| *Choose one of these or your own:* | *He is a good friend because he never says unkind things about me.* |
| | *My friend is a friend because he is always nice to me.* |

Many children, given the example prompt, chose their own improvement instead. Perhaps we have been rather too concerned in the past with marking comments being open-ended and questioning. Giving a choice of actual words or phrases acts like the beginning of a brainstorm. Children invariably think of a better or different way of writing this themselves.

The examples of work on pages 62-4 show the strategy in action in a range of classes across the country. In all cases, the improvement took no more than five minutes, often less, which was amazing to the teachers. Children appear to be highly motivated by the personal element of the 'closing the gap' prompt and the helpful structure of the comment.

When we look at the focus of *contrasts and establishing a problem* in Fig. 4 6, the misspellings of *Birmingham* and *glistened* seem trivial by comparison, yet with traditional marking, *Bihrmingham* would have been the first thing picked up by a teacher.

These pieces speak for themselves and are, in places, breathtaking. The last three examples come from an inner-city school in Tower Hamlets, where the teacher had been using this marking strategy for six months. The children's development over time is, in part, a product of the marking. Without the chance to make an improvement on the same piece of work, we will never know what children are capable of. When one piece of work is followed by a new piece of work, we are not capitalising on their ability to develop. This strategy provides a single, specific focus, rather than a general instruction to redraft.

## Making the strategy work effectively

1  Begin by telling the class that you will be changing the way you mark their writing because you realise this way will help them to progress. With older children you could even talk about the research about spelling and so on.

2  Introduce it to the whole class with a piece of work (from another class) on acetate with an overhead projector, demonstrating exactly what will happen.

3  At the beginning, go round the class, checking that they all understand what they should be doing. If they don't understand the 'closing the gap' prompt, it was the wrong one for them or they still need face-to-face marking. Remember, this strategy is designed for distance marking.

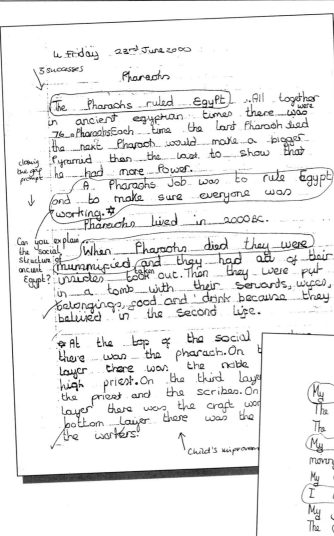

4 Friday   23rd June 2000

3 successes

Pharaohs

The Pharaohs ruled Egypt. ..All together
in ancient egyptian times there was
76 PharaohsEach time the last Pharaoh died
the next Pharaoh would make a bigger
Pyramid than the last to show that
he had more Power.

*closing the gap prompt*

A Pharaohs Job was to rule Egypt
and to make sure everyone was
working. ☆

Pharaohs lived in 2000 BC.

*Can you explain the social structure of ancient Egypt?*

When Pharaohs died they were
mummified and they had all of their
insides took out. Then they were put
in a tomb with their servants, wives,
belongings, good and drink because they
believed in the second life.

☆ At the top of the social
there was the pharaoh. On t
layer there was the noble
high priest. On the third Lay
the priest and the scribes. On
layer there was the craft wor
bottom Layer there was the
the workers!

↑ *Child's improvem*

**Fig. 4.3 Learning intention: To know what a pharaoh is and to understand their importance in Ancient Egypt**

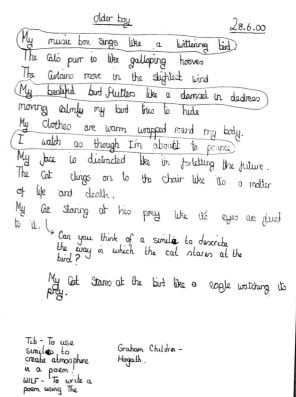

older boy                    28.6.00

My music box sings like a twittering bird
The Cats purr is like galloping hooves
The Curtains move in the slightest wind
My beautiful bird flutters like a damsel in dedress
moving calmly my bird tries to hide
My Clothes are warm wrapped round my body.
I watch as though I'm about to pounce
My face is distracted like in foretelling the future.
The Cat clings on to the chair like its a matter
of life and death.
My Cat staring at his prey like its eyes are glued
to it. ↘ *Can you think of a simile to describe
the way in which the cat stares at the
bird?*

My Cat stares at the bird like a eagle watching its
prey.

Tib - To use
similes to
create atmosphere
in a poem!
WILF - To write a
poem using The

Graham Children -
Hogath.

**Fig. 4.4 Using similes to create atmosphere**

*Fig. 4.5 Learning intention: To establish a 'problem' and use contrasts*

The wind howled viciously while the two children with eyes that glittered with anger, waited impatiently for the Killer. Peter looked across the road and saw a fire burning warmly.

"You don't think he's backing out do you?" asked Peter. The clock struck 9.00pm.

"He is supposed to be here by now!" bellowed Lucy.

[ Something jarred and caught Peter's attention. A dark figure's shadow skimmed across the cold, stone walls. Peter could hear his rythmatic footsteps........ ]  Problem achieved

Mikki if you are trying to contrast the two childrens personalities you need to make it obvious to the reader not just by what they say — so if L bellowed what will P do?

whispered nervously
asked fearfully.

would prefer apprehensively.
"...on't think he's backing out do you?" asked
apprehensively.

Learning Intention: to write an opening paragraph which introduces the 'Problem' and uses contrasts.

circles are successes

It was a bitter night in Birmingham. The old/grey walls glistned in the moonlight. There was a blanket of frost covering the whole car park, it was as if the whole place was a crystal. Max and Jenny had escaped from their beds to catch the culprit — Mr Pedding. Abruptly, a loud, curdling screech invaded the still quietness. Max spun around to see a huge bird, bigger than an eagle, bigger even than a full grown human being. It's dark shadowy figure came lumbering towards them, getting closer and closer. Before they knew it, the creature had snatched Jenny and sped off with her while Max watched in horror, speechless and motionless.

*(closing the gap prompt)*

Could you have inserted a contrast — bird = huge children = ?

This would have served to emphasise how big the bird was (big in size and power over the children) in comparison to the children.

↓ Child's improvement

Max spun around to see a huge bird, bigger than an eagle, dwarfing the delicate children, making them seem inadequate. (3 minutes)

*Fig. 4.6 Learning intention: To write an opening paragraph which introduces a problem and uses contrasts*

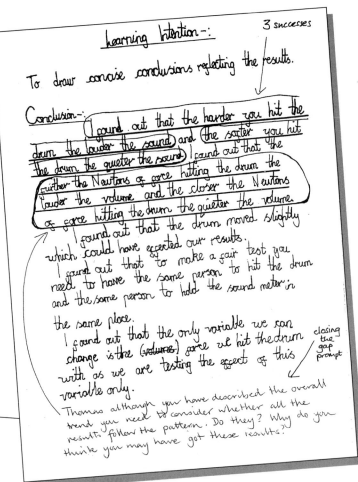

Learning Intention-:

To draw concise conclusions reflecting the results.

3 successes

Conclusion-:
I found out that the harder you hit the drum the louder the sound and the softer you hit the drum the quieter the sound. I found out that the further the Newtons of force hitting the drum the louder the volume and the closer the Newtons of force hitting the drum the quieter the volume. I found out that the drum moved slightly which could have effected our results.
I found out that to make a fair test you need to have the same person to hit the drum and the same person to hold the sound meter in the same place.
I found out that the only variable we can change is the (volume) force we hit the drum with as we are testing the effect of this variable only.

closing the gap prompt

Thomas although you have described the overall trend you need to consider whether all the results follow the pattern. Do they? Why do you think you may have got these results?

Child's improvement

Learning Intention-:

To draw concise conclusions.

The final 2 results don't actually follow the pattern of a gradual overall increase. When I looked at the results of the trials I noticed that the results for trials 1,2,3 did not increase as much as they should. This might have been because when we moved the sound meter away from the drum we were changing more than 1 variable. Not only were we testing how the force we hit the drum affected the volume but also how distance can affect the volume.

(5 minutes)

*Fig. 4.7 Learning intention: To draw concise conclusions reflecting the results*

*4*    Some children sometimes simply answer the question you write, rather than replacing the arrowed phrase (e.g. 'closing the gap' prompt: *Could you compare the price difference in a clearer way?* Child's improvement: *If Fairy was £2, mine would be £1.50*). To stop this happening, include the words *'Replace this phrase'* or similar, or simply explain to the child.

*5*    The teacher needs to read the work all the way through first, or the highlights can be ill-considered and/or there is a temptation to start correcting spellings! If it seems difficult to find three highlights, this is a cue for face-to-face discussion with the child. The work was probably either inappropriate for that child or not enough was generated in the time, or distance marking is inappropriate.

*6*    If the 'improvement' is not actually an improvement, the problem nearly always lies with the quality of the 'closing the gap' prompt.

## *Developing the strategy*

Teachers using this strategy for even a short time (two weeks) have described a variety of spin-offs. The coded marking lends itself to self- and paired marking. Children start to guess which highlights the teacher would choose, presenting a clear opportunity for the child to choose their own highlights. Paired marking with this strategy produces high-quality dialogue, especially if the children work together on each other's work.

Teachers find themselves using this strategy when marking children's work face-to-face. The 'closing the gap' prompt might be oral with younger children, but the strategy is equally effective with face-to-face marking.

Teachers have found it useful in other subject areas whenever writing takes place, as was illustrated by the Science writing (Fig. 4.7).

With closed tasks, where there are right or wrong answers – such as in a comprehension or spelling exercise – there is no advantage or sense in using three highlights. Ticks and crosses are still appropriate. However, teachers have found that it can still be useful to use the arrow and a 'closing the gap' prompt for one of the mistakes.

Mathematics has been less successful with coded marking, because sometimes children get all the answers right. Clearly the coded marking would apply well to open-ended problem-solving, but with 'closed' tasks it is more limiting. When all the answers are right, some teachers have used an arrow and an 'extending the gap' prompt – an extension idea.

## Finding time to do this

Firstly, you have to believe that this is a vital aspect of children's learning and development, in order to make the time. Teachers have mainly taken the first five to ten minutes in the morning or afternoon or the beginning of the Literacy Hour, before the children start today's lesson. With the latter, other parts of the Literacy lesson will need to be cut short. All Literacy Consultants I have spoken to have said how 'delighted' they would be to see this happening: the improvement time is, after all, reading and writing. On one day the text-level work might be shorter, on another the independent work, on another the plenary and so on, so that the same part is not curtailed each time. The closer to the lesson the work is returned, the better it is for the child, but teachers have found that children refocus relatively easily when they are reminded of the work. While most children are dealing with their improvement, there is an opportunity to speak to those children who need face-to-face intervention.

Whether this strategy is more or less demanding than current marking practice depends of course on the teacher's current practice. For many teachers it is less work, because they have been marking so many aspects, but for some it might mean more. However, the benefits make it worthwhile even if this is the case. Clearly, it would be unmanageable to mark *every* piece of writing in this way, so schools have tended to agree a minimum number to receive this kind of quality marking.

# The impact of focused marking

## The impact on children

- Self-esteem increases as a result of children's more visible improvements.

- Children like the system and are very motivated to make their improvement.

- Children are eager to look at their marked work and enjoy looking back at previous comments.

- In one class, every child came in before school to do their 'closing the gap' improvements and talk about them. The teacher said *'This is a miracle. They usually lurk in the toilets before school.'*

- Children's writing improves, as well as the quality of their oral comments about their work.

- More able children are able to suggest 'closing the gap' comments.

- Children find it more useful than previous marking.

- Children keep looking up at the success criteria when they know the work will be marked in this way.

- Children make better connections between their work and the learning intention.

- By focusing on one thing at a time, children improve their repertoire of skills.

## *The impact on teachers*

- Teachers who have applied the marking system consistently, say that it is one of the most useful of the formative assessment strategies in enabling the teacher to see tangible results of change and in providing evidence of improvement. Other common remarks are that marking is *'much less stressful'*, the strategy is *'liberating'* and the whole thing is *'exciting'*.

- The quality of the child's improvement depends on the quality of the 'closing the gap' comment. As one teacher said, *'If you've hit that well, it works like a dream.'*

- There is a clearer purpose in marking, so teachers feel more confident and satisfied about spending time on it.

- The strategy again focuses the teacher on the learning intention of the task.

- Looking for the three highlights challenges teachers' knowledge of the learning intention and can lead to learning intentions being broken down or made clearer in planning sheets.

Comments made by teachers include the following:

> *Creating the "closing the gap" comment is the hardest part – it makes you really feel like you're being a teacher, and you do gradually improve.*

> *It has noticeably improved children's progress.*

> *It was hard to ignore spellings after so many years of marking them every time.*

> *It was much quicker to mark in this way, focusing only on the learning intention.*

> *Brighter children are asking for more "closing the gap" comments.*

## Wider implications and effects

The marking strategy, as with all other formative assessment strategies, needs to be the subject of a whole-school focus, taking parents and governors with you over a set period of time. Parents, especially, need clear communication about marking, because they have certain expectations based on their own experiences of school. We need to tell them about the research findings and explain how spelling is actually learnt, and so on. The marking had been particularly useful for parents to see at open day, because the child's improvement and what is being learnt is clearly visible.

Of all the formative assessment strategies, focused marking is probably the most challenging for teachers, because it gets right to the heart of teaching. Children's response to the teacher's oral focus and marking focus inspires teachers to persist. The purpose of marking has, for many years, been clouded by the perception – and often the reality – of inspectors' and parents' expectations, but these teachers felt realigned to the real purpose of marking: to feed back to children about their successes and improvement needs against the learning intention – a real tool for learning and improvement. As with the other formative assessment strategies, teachers using this strategy feel that they cannot go back, that their practice is now fundamentally imbued with these processes.

# A marking and feedback policy

The following draft policy was created by teachers on a number of 'Marking and Feedback' courses at the Institute of Education. It could serve as a starting point for developing your own school policy.

## MARKING AND FEEDBACK POLICY

### Mission Statement

We believe feedback and marking should provide constructive feedback to every child, focusing on success and improvement needs against learning intentions; enabling children to become reflective learners and helping them to close the gap between current and desired performance.

### Principles

Marking and feedback should:

■ Be manageable for teachers.

■ Relate to learning intentions, which need to be shared with children.

■ Involve all adults working with children in the classroom.

■ Give children opportunities to become aware of and reflect on their learning needs.

■ Give recognition and appropriate praise for achievement.

■ Give clear strategies for improvement.

■ Allow specific time for children to read, reflect and respond to marking.

■ Involve children in the same process (whether oral or written), to ensure equity across subjects and abilities.

■ Take an ipsative approach (where attainment is based on that person's previous attainment) within the context of marking towards the learning intention.

■ Respond to individual learning needs, marking face-to-face with some and at a distance for others.

■ Inform future planning and individual target setting.

■ Be accessible to children.

■ Use consistent codes throughout the school.

■ Ultimately be seen by children as positive in improving their learning.

■ Encourage and teach children to self-mark wherever possible.

## Strategies

### Summative feedback/marking

This usually consists of ticks and crosses and is associated with closed tasks or exercises. Wherever possible, children should self-mark or the work should be marked as a class or in groups.

### Formative feedback/marking

With oral feedback, in the course of a lesson, teachers' comments to children should focus firstly on issues about the learning intention and secondly, and in a whisper, on other features.

*Quality marking*

Not all pieces of work can be 'quality marked'. Teachers need to decide whether work will simply be acknowledged or given detailed attention.

Wherever the task is open or narrative, feedback should focus first and foremost on the learning intention of the task. The emphasis in marking should be on both success against the learning intention and improvement needs against the learning intention. Focused comment should help the child in 'closing the gap' between what they have achieved and what they could have achieved (e.g. *'What else could you say about the prince?'*, *'Say something about the prince's personality'*, *'Try one of these words: handsome, elegant, arrogant'*). With English narrative writing, codes can save time and make the feedback more accessible to the child: highlight three things (maybe two or even one per child with younger children) which are best against the learning intention and put an arrow where improvement against the learning intention could take place, including a 'closing the gap' comment. Where codes are inappropriate, success and improvement should be pointed out verbally or in written form. Useful 'closing the gap' comments are:

■ A **reminder** prompt (e.g. *'What else could you say here?'*).

■ A **scaffolded** prompt (e.g. *'What was the dog's tail doing?'*, *'The dog was angry so he...'*, *'Describe the expression on the dog's face'*).

■ An **example** prompt (e.g. *'Choose one of these or your own: He ran round in circles looking for the rabbit/The dog couldn't believe his eyes'*).

## Secretarial features

Spelling, punctuation, grammar, etc., should not be asked for in every piece of narrative writing, because children cannot effectively focus on too many things in one space of time. When work is finished, ask children to check for things *they know are wrong in their work* when they read it through. They should not be told to correct all spellings, or they are likely to write further misspellings or waste time looking words up.

Only give children feedback about those things you have asked them to pay attention to. This will mean that some aspects of writing are unmarked, but over time will be marked.

## Self-marking

Children should self-evaluate wherever possible. Children can identify their own three successes and look for improvement points. The plenary can then focus on this process as a way of analysing the learning.

## Shared marking

Using one piece of work from a child in another class to mark as a class, using OHP, at regular intervals, models the marking process and teaches particular points at the same time.

Another strategy is to show two pieces of levelled work, with the same title, and discuss their differences.

## Paired marking

Before ends of lessons, children should sometimes be asked to mark narrative work in pairs. The following points are important:

■ Paired marking should not be introduced until Key Stage 2, unless teachers feel younger children are ready for this.

■ Children need to be trained to do this, through modelling with the whole class, watching the paired marking in action.

■ Ground rules (e.g. listening, interruptions, confidentiality, etc.) should be decided, then put up as a poster.

■ Children should, alternately, point out what they like first, holding the highlighter pen, and then suggest ways to improve the piece, but only against the learning intention and not spellings, etc. The 3:1 success to improvement ratio should be followed, to avoid over-criticism.

■ Pairings need to be based on someone you trust – best decided by teacher.

■ Pairings should be ability based, of two middle, two brighter or one middle and one lower together.

■ Encourage a dialogue between children rather than taking turns to be the 'teacher': they should discuss each other's work together (e.g. *'I think this bit really shows how that character feels, what do you think?'*)

**Organisation**

■ The first 5–10 minutes of a lesson should, wherever possible, be used to get around the class to establish understanding and act on it where the work is too easy or too difficult.

■ Where possible, children should be encouraged to self-mark.

■ Set less work, especially in literacy and mathematics, so that time can be allowed to go through work and mark as a class.

■ Wherever class discussion takes place, feedback is given orally. Notes might also be necessary to inform future planning as a result of the discussion findings.

■ Children need to have some feedback about their work, but flexibility is important, depending on the nature of the task and the time available.

■ Distance marking should be accessible to children and manageable for teachers. Use codes against learning intentions wherever possible.

■ When work has been distance marked, time should be given for children to read and then make one focused improvement based on the improvement suggestion (linked with the arrow when codes are used). In order for the marking to be formative, the information must be used and acted on by the children.

Date agreed:

Date reviewed:

**************************

**INSET ideas**

1.  Inform teachers, parents and governors about the research findings about feedback. Use *Inside the Black Box* and *Beyond the Black Box* for good quotes and bullet points, as well as sections from this chapter.
2.  Take oral feedback first and get teachers to try this in the classroom, with a feedback meeting to share findings.
3.  At a staff meeting, introduce the focused coded marking strategy, showing the examples of children's work from this chapter. Look carefully at each one, discussing the highlights, arrows, 'closing the gap' prompts and children's improvements.
4.  In the same meeting ask teachers, in pairs, to mark some English work in the same way, firstly given photocopies of the same piece of work and secondly with work they have brought to the meeting. Share highlights and 'closing the gap' prompts and discuss and work on these together.
5.  Get teachers to trial the approach for half a term, before a feedback meeting to discuss issues. Bring work to the feedback meeting to share examples of children's improvements.
6.  Collect all the ways in which spelling is taught and learnt in school as evidence for disbelievers!

# 5 Target setting

## The current context

Never before has there been such an obsession with target setting in education! To begin with, targets were suggested within the school improvement context, and used as a vehicle for focusing development on particular issues, at school, class and pupil levels. However, the emphasis changed when the government announced national targets to be met by 2002. Pressure has cascaded from government to LEAs, to schools, to pupils, as everyone is accountable – their success measured simply by the number of Level 4s attained. Because the final focus is on SAT results, teachers now find themselves in an unrivalled 'high-stakes' testing regime.

High-stakes testing exists when the stakes are high for those involved in the process. In the current situation the stakes are high for teachers and schools, not children. Children's subsequent schooling is not affected by SAT results, unlike the old '11-plus' exams or Common Entrance exams, yet many children now talk about SAT results as if they will have a personal consequence. In the panic to attain Level 4s, many schools report levels every year to parents, even though the statutory requirement is to report only at the end of Years 2 and 6.

Research on grading pupils shows that children are less motivated and often demoralised when they are continually compared to each other. They need to know the criteria for the next level above, but they do not need to know what that level is called. If children are given a list of criteria, without the title 'Level 2a' for instance, they experience maximum motivation and focus and have no interest in comparing their performance and perceived ability with others. Parents have the right to know how well a child is doing – whether they are average, below or above, in relation to external criteria – but the idea that they must be told the level of the child's attainment at any time is a myth. The statutory requirements were created deliberately to stop children and parents getting demoralised by children taking two years to move up a level, which is the norm.

We need to remember that, in the end, the number of level 4s attained will not represent our ultimate aims for education in the twenty-first century, but a bare minimum standard of those elements of learning which are *easy to test*. As Sir Richard Livingstone said, 60 years ago:

' *The test of a successful education is not the amount of knowledge that a pupil takes away from a school but his appetite to know and his capacity to learn. If the school sends out children with the desire for knowledge and some idea of how to acquire and use it, it will have done its work. Too many leave school with the appetite killed and the mind loaded with undigested lumps of information.* '
(cited in Abbott,1999)

# Individual target setting

There are three elements to target setting at pupil level: **quantitative** tracking of targets from year to year (number crunching), individual **qualitative** targets (written in words) and **non-recorded** targets.

## *Quantitative targets*

Most schools have a computer program that allows them to enter children's levels each year. Pupil progress can then be tracked each year to see whether each child is on course and, if not, what action should follow. One school's procedures can be seen in Fig. 5.1. The QCA 'non-statutory SATs', or optional tests, are the most common vehicle for generating levels each year from Year 3 to Year 5. Many schools enter other data so that they can analyse performance against key factors, such as race or gender. One school's data analysis yielded the information shown in Fig. 5.2, for

---

POLICY FOR TRACKING PUPIL PROGRESS
USING ASSESSMENT MANAGER

**Purpose:** To use the results of regular standardised testing, teacher predictions and assessment to inform planning, teaching, and the target setting process.

**Aim:** To collect and utilise effectively data relating to pupil progress through KS2

**Method:**

- **ON ENTRY: Record KS1 Teacher Assessments and test results for English Maths and Science.**
- **ANNUALLY SEPTEMBER: Give Y3 teachers KS1 assessments for their classes. Give Y4, Y5 and Y6 class teachers previous year's NFER NVR scores and QCA English and Maths scores from previous year.**
- **OCTOBER Give staff record sheets for target setting and predictions. Request return by Half Term Autumn.**
- **Record on marksheets asap in preparation for discussion with LEA and Governors to set targets for Y5 to achieve in EOKS2 SATS, and discussion with staff re targetting for ALS/ Booster Groups or for targetted teaching.**
- **ANNUALLY JANUARY: Conduct NFER Non Verbal Reasoning tests in all years within first three weeks of the Spring Term. Record scores.**
- **ANNUALLY MAY : Y3,4,5 complete appropriate QCA tests in Maths and English. Record Scores. Y6 teachers complete Teacher Assessments and children complete SATS tests in English Maths and Science.**
- **ANNUALLY JULY: Record levels. Record marks within levels.**
- **BY END OF TERM: Compare predictions, targets and achievements for all classes by subject. Produce analysis of SATS results for Y6 and other interested staff by gender and registration group. Use in discussion with Governors and LEA if required.**
- **Record KS1 for new intake.**

**This strategy complements the existing school policy on Assessment and Record Keeping, and assists the Headteacher, Governors and Senior Management team in monitoring standards. It will be trialled 2000/2001 and reviewed in the light of experience and/or statutory requirement.**

*Fig. 5.1 Using a computer program for tracking summative assessment*

instance, which shows that girls in that year were doing less well in mathematics and science.

A table like that in Fig. 5.3 (shown here with children's names omitted) enables each child to be carefully tracked.

# Key Stage Two SATs Results 1998 (in % terms)

## General

|         | 1 | 2 | 3    | 4    | 5    |
|---------|---|---|------|------|------|
| English | 0 | 0 | 11.1 | 59.2 | 29.6 |
| Maths   | 0 | 0 | 14.8 | 44.4 | 40.7 |
| Science | 0 | 0 | 3.7  | 48.1 | 48.1 |

**In English 88.8% of pupils achieved Level 4 or above**
**In Maths 85.1% of pupils achieved Level 4 or above**
**In Science 96.2% of pupils achieved Level 4 or above**

In **English** it has been possible this year to give each pupil a Level for Reading and for Writing:
In **Reading** 92.5% of pupils achieved Level 4 or above (29.6% achieved Level 5)
In **Writing** 66.6% of pupils achieved Level 4 or above (29.6% achieved Level 5)
In **Mathematics** it has been possible to give pupils a Level for Tests A & B and a Level for the Mental Arithmetic Test:
In Tests A & B 85.1% of pupils achieved Level 4 or above (51.8% achieved Level 5)
In the Mental Arithmetic Test 66.6% achieved Level 4 or more (33.3% achieved Level 5)

## EAL pupils

90% of EAL children achieved Level 4 or above in English (22.5% achieved Level 5)
81% of EAL children achieved Level 4 or above in Maths (36% achieved Level 5)
94.5% of EAL children achieved Level 4 or above in Science (40.5% achieved Level 5)

## Gender

91.2% of Girls achieved Level 4 or above in English (38% achieved Level 5)
85.2% of Boys achieved Level 4 or above in English (21.3% achieved Level 5)

76% of Girls achieved Level 4 or above in Maths (30.4% achieved Level 5)
85.2% of Boys achieved Level 4 or above in Maths (49.4% achieved Level 5)

91.2% of Girls achieved Level 4 or above in Science (38% achieved Level 5)
100% of Boys achieved Level 4 or above in Science (56.8% achieved Level 5)

*Fig. 5.2 Analysis of Key Stage 2 assessment data*

What matters, of course, is what you *do* with this data. It needs to be the subject of senior management scrutiny at ends or beginnings of years, along with a breakdown of SAT results, to decide possible staff INSET targets, class targets and teacher targets. Pupil targets need to be both bottom-up and top-down: tailor-made to suit each child, but within the context of the level above the level they are currently achieving.

| RELIGION | EO | G | Maths | | | | | Reading | | | | | Writing | | | | | Spelling | | | | |
|---|---|---|---|---|---|---|---|---|---|---|---|---|---|---|---|---|---|---|---|---|---|---|
| | | | Yr.2 | Yr.3 | Yr.4 | Yr.5 | Yr.6 | Yr.2 | Yr.3 | Yr.4 | Yr.5 | Yr.6 | Yr.2 | Yr.3 | Yr.4 | Yr.5 | Yr.6 | Yr.2 | Yr.3 | Yr.4 | Yr.5 | Yr.6 |
| MUSLIM | B'DESHI | B | 1 | 2c | 2a | 3b | 4 | 2c | 3c | 3b | 3a | 4 | 1 | 2c | 2a | 3b | 4 | bl2 | 2 | A | | |
| MUSLIM | B'DESHI | B | 2b | 2a | 2b | 3c | 4 | 1 | 2b | 3c | 3a | 4 | 1 | 2b | 2a | 3b | 4 | bl2 | 2 | 3 | | |
| XTIAN | BAFR | G | 2c | 2c | 2b | 3c | 4 | 2a | 3a | 3b | 4a | 5 | 2c | 3c | 3b | 4a | 5+ | 2 | 3 | 3 | | |
| MUSLIM | B'DESHI | G | 1 | bl2 | 2b | 2a | 4 | W | bl2 | 2b | 3b | 4 | W | bl2 | 2c | 2a | 3+ | bl2 | bl2 | 2 | | |
| MUSLIM | B'DESHI | G | 1 | bl2 | 2b | 3b | 4 | 2b | 2a | 3b | 3+ | 4 | 2c | 2a | 3b | 4a | 5+ | 2 | 3 | 4 | | |
| MUSLIM | B'DESHI | G | 1 | 2b | 2c | 2a | 3 | W | bl2 | 2a | 3b | 4 | W | bl2 | 2c | 3a | 4 | bl2 | bl2 | bl2 | | |
| MUSLIM | B'DESHI | G | 2b | 3c | 3b | 4 | 4+ | 2b | 3a | 3b | 4 | 5 | 2c | 3a | 4 | 5 | 5+ | 2 | 4 | 4 | | |
| | CHINESE | B | 3 | 4 | 4+ | 5 | 5+ | 2a | 4 | 4+ | 5 | 5+ | 2c | 3b | 3a | 4b | 5 | 2 | 3 | 4 | | |
| XTIAN | NIGERIAN | B | 1 | 2b | 3c | 4b | 4+ | 2b | 2a | 3b | 4a | 5 | 1 | 2b | 2a | 3b | 4 | bl2 | 2 | 3 | | |
| XTIAN | BRIT | B | 1 | bl2 | bl2 | 2a | 3 | 1 | bl2 | 2c | 2b | 3 | 1 | bl2 | bl2 | 2b | 3+ | bl2 | bl2 | bl2 | | |
| XTIAN | BRIT | B | 3 | 2a | 2a | 3b | 4 | 2c | 3c | 3a | 4 | 4+ | 2b | 2b | 2a | 3b | 4 | bl2 | 2 | 2 | | |
| MUSLIM | B'DESHI | G | 2c | 2a | 2a | 3b | 4 | 2b | 2b | 2a | 3b | 4+ | 2c | A | 2a | 3b | 4 | 2 | 3 | 2 | | |
| MUSLIM | B'DESHI | B | W | bl2 | bl2 | 2 | 3 | | bl2 | bl2 | 2c | 3 | | bl2 | bl2 | 2c | 3 | | bl2 | A | | |
| MUSLIM | B'DESHI | B | 1 | 2b | 2b | 3a | 4 | 1 | bl2 | 2c | 2+ | 3+ | W | bl2 | bl2 | 2b | 3 | bl2 | bl2 | bl2 | | |
| XTIAN | BRIT | G | 1 | 2c | 2c | 2a | 3 | 1 | bl2 | bl2 | 2+ | 3+ | W | bl2 | bl2 | 2b | 3 | bl2 | bl2 | bl2 | | |
| XTIAN | BRIT | G | 2a | 3c | 3c | 4 | 5 | 2a | 3a | 4+ | 5 | 5+ | 2b | 3a | 3a | 4b | 5+ | 2 | 3 | 3 | | |
| MUSLIM | B'DESHI | G | 2b | 2a | 3c | 4 | 5 | 2b | 3c | 3c | 3a | 4+ | 2b | 2a | 3b | 4a | 5+ | 2 | A | 2 | | |
| MUSLIM | MOROC | B | | 2c | 2a | 3b | 4 | | bl2 | bl2 | 2b | 3+ | | bl2 | 2a | 2b | 3+ | | bl2 | A | | |
| XTIAN | BRIT | G | 3c | 3c | 4+ | 5 | 5+ | 4 | 4 | 4+ | 5 | 5+ | | 3a | 4 | 5 | 5+ | | 3 | 4 | | |
| MUSLIM | B'DESHI | B | 1 | bl2 | 2c | 2a | 3+ | W | bl2 | 2b | 3a | 4 | W | bl2 | A | 2b | 3+ | bl2 | bl2 | 2 | | |
| MUSLIM | SOMALI | B | | bl2 | bl2 | 2c | 3+ | | bl2 | bl2 | 2c | 3 | | bl2 | bl2 | 2c | 3+ | | bl2 | A | | |
| XTIAN | NIGERIAN | B | 3 | 2a | 3c | 4a | 5 | 1 | bl2 | 2c | 3c | 4 | 1 | bl2 | 2c | 2a | 3+ | bl2 | 2 | bl2 | | |
| XTIAN | NIGERIAN | B | 2b | 2b | 2b | 2a | 3+ | 1 | 2c | 2b | 3a | 4+ | 1 | A | bl2 | 2a | 3+ | bl2 | 2 | 2 | | |
| MUSLIM | B'DESHI | B | W | A | bl2 | bl2 | bl2 | W | bl2 | bl2 | bl2 | bl2 | W | bl2 | bl2 | 1 | 1 | X | bl2 | bl2 | | |
| MUSLIM | B'DESHI | G | 3 | 3b | 3a | 4b | 5 | 2b | 3c | 4+ | 5 | 5+ | 2c | 2a | 3b | 4a | 5+ | 2 | 3 | 3 | | |
| MUSLIM | B'DESHI | G | 1 | bl2 | 2c | 2a | 3+ | 1 | bl2 | 2c | 2a | 3+ | W | bl2 | bl2 | 2a | 3+ | bl2 | 2 | A | | |
| MUSLIM | B'DESHI | B | 1 | bl2 | bl2 | bl2 | bl2 | W | bl2 | bl2 | bl2 | bl2 | W | bl2 | bl2 | 1 | 1 | X | bl2 | bl2 | | |
| MUSLIM | B'DESHI | B | 1 | 2c | 2b | 3a | 4 | 1 | bl2 | bl2 | 2a | 3+ | 1 | bl2 | bl2 | 2a | 3+ | 1 | bl2 | A | | |
| MUSLIM | B'DESHI | B | N | bl2 | 2c | 2a | 5+ | 1 | 2c | bl2 | 2a | 3+ | 1 | A | 2c | 2a | 3+ | bl2 | 2 | A | | |
| XTIAN | BRIT | G | | 4 | 4+ | 5+ | | | 4+ | 5 | | | | 4 | 5 | 5+ | | | 3 | | | |

Year 5 Pupil Statistics (30 children)
50% are eligible for free school meals
27% are summer born
30% have had extended leave at some point in their schooling
50% are identified as having special educational needs
80% have English as an additional language

*Fig. 5.3 Year-on-year results*

# Qualitative pupil targets

My main focus here is on Writing targets, for two reasons: firstly, writing is an area of perceived weakness, and secondly, teachers have found that writing skills which have been 'targeted' can be easily practised by children in the course of their lessons. Maths targets, on the other hand, have, since the onset of the Numeracy Strategy, been seen as very difficult to work with. This is because children's individual maths targets cannot necessarily be practised during a Numeracy lesson. Even mental maths targets suffer from this, as the maths covered in the 'warm-up' might never cover the content of some children's targets. Creating maths targets for homework seems a good idea, but this falls down when parental support is variable. It seems, then, that we might have been trying to create maths targets for the sake of it, when it is, in fact, unworkable. More useful, perhaps, would be whole-class targets, displayed on a poster, of the 'using and applying' elements of mathematics, which are the subject of a class focus every two weeks, say, regardless of the maths content at the time.

One of the key recommendations derived from research is that we must keep some kind of *ipsative* assessment in place in our classrooms. To explain this in the context of other forms of referencing:

■ **criterion referencing** is where the child's attainment is measured against external criteria, as in the National Curriculum;

■ **norm referencing** is where the child's attainment is compared with other children's attainment (creating below-average, average or above-average categories);

■ **ipsative referencing** is where the child's attainment is measured against his or her own previous attainment.

Characteristics of ipsative referencing are increased motivation and a rise in self-esteem. Black and Wiliam saw this as crucial, because the research shows that the key to successful learning is to have a high self-esteem. The most obvious vehicle for ipsative referencing in the current context seems to be individual target setting, in which manageability is of course a prime concern.

## Visibility: the power of the visual image again

Targets need to be visible while children are working, so cards or flaps seem to work best – cards in a box on each table or flaps attached to the top edge of the back cover of children's writing books. Wherever the writing goes, the card or flap goes with it, so the teacher is constantly reminded of the child's target and is able to consider on a day-to-day basis whether or not the target has been met. Because these are visible during lessons, the target is known and remembered, by the child and the teacher.

There are probably many systems for the development of targets on cards or flaps, but one is outlined here:

The teacher writes one target at a time on the child's card. The choice is made by either:

1    Asking the child what they think their next target should be (much more likely if they are fully involved in sharing learning intentions, pupil self-evaluation and marking against the learning intention, as in the previous chapters). It is a good idea to have a list of the child's criteria (the level above their current level) written in 'child-speak' and pasted into the back of their writing book. They have this for the year and can consult it at any time to look ahead at what they think might be a good target. Remember to remove the heading (e.g. Level 2a) to avoid comparisons, and so on, as previously mentioned.

*or*

2    The teacher looks at the child's writing and decides the next target based on what she sees. This only really works for young children where their needs are obvious.

*or*

3    The teacher looks at the sub-level above the child's current attainment and chooses a target from that list. The Writing criteria can be broken down into sub-levels with 'target prompts' in a form which can be written on a child's writing target card or flap. Teachers find this extremely useful.

Fig. 5.4 contains examples of Writing targets with 'target prompts' and in 'child-speak', both of which might be used as a starting point for developing a school's own versions.

## Target prompts

**Sufficient detail is given to engage the reader.**

- Remember to think about who you are writing for and make it as interesting for them as you can.

**Narrative or non-narrative form is used with some consistency.**

- Remember the writing we have looked at in shared writing when you do your own writing and remember what made it good.
- Think of things you have read when you do your own writing

**Variation is evident in sentence structure with some extended sentences extended and linked with connectives other than 'and'.**

- Make some sentences long and some short to make your writing more interesting.
- Try to use **but, then, so** or **because** in between two sentences or instead of **and**, if it will make the sentence more interesting.

**Word choices are varied and sometimes ambitious.**

- Try to use interesting words in your writing, to describe people or things.
- Read your work and choose the words you think are the most effective.
- Try to change two words in your writing for more interesting or better words.

**There is evidence of some sentence punctuation.**

- Try to have 4/5/6 sentences in your writing which have a capital letter at the beginning and a full stop at the end.
- Check your writing to see if you could put in a comma, a question mark or an exclamation mark.

Spelling ...

Handwriting ...

## Expressing targets in 'child-speak'

**I am learning to:**

- write stories that make sense all the way through
- write a story in which there is more than one person or animal
- write a story in which several things happen
- use interesting and different words in my writing
- use **'but'**, **'then'** and other words to join sentences
- use capital letters and full stops for most of my sentences
- spell correctly on my own easy words that I use a lot
- use letter patterns to help me spell words (patterns like **oo**, **ck** and **nt**)
- use rhymes to help me spell words (**call, fall, ball, tall**)
- make sure **g p j q y** all sit on the line
- make sure **t l k f d b** are all taller than the other letters
- make sure I don't put capital letters in the middle of words

*Fig. 5.4 Making the Writing targets accessible to children. Working towards Writing level 2b*

Many LEAs have created such lists. These examples come from Essex and Nottinghamshire LEAs and a school in Bedfordshire: the full versions, covering Levels 1 to 6, can be accessed from the *Unlocking Formative Assessment* page on www.hodderheadline.co.uk

Children need to be told what it means to meet a target. It is best to say something like *'You've met your target when you and I believe you will always be able to do that thing.'* It does not work to try to keep track of how many times a child has demonstrated their target, because this creates unmanageable paperwork.

It is a good idea to introduce a symbol (e.g. T), which the children write at the bottom of their work if they think they have met their target. The children are told that after they have put the 'T' it may be a few days before the teacher sees them about their target. This gives the teacher a 'buffer' and allows time to decide when to see the child about their target. Similarly, the symbol can be used by the teacher to show children that she thinks the target has been met. This could be done during marking, while working with a group or while walking around the class.

The meeting with the child needs to be short, or the system will be unmanageable. The three strategies listed above make the process of choosing the next target efficient. If the current target has not been fully met, the best strategy seems to be to write a new target for the child which shows them explicitly how to meet their current target (e.g. *Use 'but' and 'then' in another three pieces of writing*).

## Getting the targets right

Feedback from teachers using these systems shows that children are highly motivated by their targets and make better progress than before. However, there are two possible negatives:

1   If the teacher is too generous with the targets, they can turn over too quickly and the system becomes unmanageable. If this happens, children need to be told that their targets will be slightly more challenging and will take longer to achieve.

2  If the target is too general, it becomes unachievable for the child, for example *'Try to remember to use capital letters and full stops'* will be unachievable for a child who is not currently using capital letters and full stops, whereas a focused target such as *'In each piece of writing, try to write four sentences which have a capital letter at the beginning and a full stop at the end'* is more likely to be realised.

The target needs to be **quantified** by number or letter. For instance:

- ■ Try to use *but* and *then* in-between some of your sentences.

- ■ Do not use a rubber for the next five pieces of writing.

- ■ Remember to have *b* and *d* the right way round.

The quantifying provides a strategy for the child. In checking for four sentences, for instance, the child often then creates another one – a 'snowball effect' has been noticed by many teachers. Interestingly, it is possible to see the link between the style of the success criteria of a lesson ('What I'm Looking For') and the style of a well-quantified target.

The target cards provide a record, are passed on to the next teacher and are useful to share with parents. Keeping Writing targets means that post-Dearing-style individual portfolios of sampled writing become unnecessary and comparatively unhelpful.

## Non-recorded targets

These have been mentioned in Chapter 3, but it is important to remember their presence. During self-evaluation sessions, children often set themselves targets as a result of what they discover about themselves (e.g. *'I've realised I need to learn my tables because that was why I had difficulty'*). As a result of focused marking, children often set themselves mental targets as they realise how much better their improvement makes their work. There is also evidence of this in paired marking. Teachers are continually setting themselves targets as they learn what works, what doesn't work, and what makes things work better. We simply need to acknowledge the existence of non-recorded target setting as a natural process for a confident learner.

**Name:** Roman    Year 3

**TARGET CARD**    **WRITING**

| Date | Target | Achieved |
|------|--------|----------|
| 9/11/99 | To write 3 sentences in the first 5 minutes of working. | ✓ (4x) |
| 8/12/99 | To do 3 lines of joined and leave a space in writing between | ✓✓✓✓ (4x) |

**Name:** Ross    Year 3

**TARGET CARD**    **WRITING**

| Date | Target | Achieved |
|------|--------|----------|
| 9/11 | Write a capital letter at the beginning of every sentence (5x) | ✓✓✓✓ |
| 25/11 | Make sure the words are on the line and write on every other line. (5x) | ✓✓✓✓ |
| 26/1/00 | To start each line writing at the margin (5x) | ✓✓✓ |
| | Use 2 interesting adjectives in a | ✓✓ |

**NATALIE**

| Date set | Target | Date achieved |
|----------|--------|---------------|
| 7/11/99 | Make sure your capital letters are clear and larger than your lower case letters. | 18/01/00 |
| 18/01/00 | Check that you have used commas in sentences where you have written more than one phrase, or if you have written a list | 7/02/00 |
| 7/02/00 | In creative writing underline and use a thesaurus to | |
| 8/03/00 | To complete a given piece during our Literacy Hour | |
| 11/04/00 | Read through your finished writing you can replace any 'and' such as 'but', 'when', 'also', 'when' or 'although'. | |
| 25/05/00 | Remember to use an exclama someone is angry, amazed or Exclamation Marks →!!! | |

**HANNAH**

| Date set | Target | Date achieved |
|----------|--------|---------------|
| 2/11/99 | When you have decided on the style of your story (eg. legend, fairy tale) keep reading it over to make sure you are staying in your chosen style. | 7/12/99 |
| 7/12/99 | Check that you have used paragraphs to separate new subjects or events. If have left them out put paragraphs | 17/01/00 |
| 17/01/00 | | 26/01/00 |
| 26/01/00 | | 03/00 |

**Name:** Cady-Ann    Year 6

**TARGET CARD**    **WRITING**    Frequency

| Date | Target | Achieved | |
|------|--------|----------|-|
| 8.9.99 | To write a story with a clear beginning, middle and end | ||| | 3x |
| | To proof read work for spellings and capitals (x5) | !!!!! | 8x |
| 12.10.99 | Have a clear B.M.E in 3 paragraphs, with one main problem to solve | ||| | 2x |
| 8.1.00 | | !!!!! | 5x |
| 27.2.00 | Develop surprise by using hooks in the story | !!! | 3x |
| 13.3.00 | To set out direct speech correctly (3x) | !!! | 3x |
| 24.4.00 | To have one good, one bad character in my next story | | | 4x |
| 19.5.00 | To have one big event in my next story | | | 2x |
| 27.5.00 | To begin my next 2 stories with speech | || | 3x |
| 16.6.00 | To use a range of connectors in my writing (3x) | ||| | 3x |

**Name:** Natalie    Year 6

**TARGET CARD**    **WRITING**

| Date | Target | Achieved | |
|------|--------|----------|-|
| 8.9.99 | To include more description in my writing | |||| | 4x |
| 9.10.99 | To include similes and metaphors in my next 2 stories | || | 4x |
| 2.11.99 | To develop my character in a story through direct speech | ||| | 2x |
| 18.01.00 | To set my information out in clear paragraphs | ||| | 3x |
| 20.2.00 | To use a range of connectors in my writing | ||| | 3x |
| 15.3.00 | To begin my next 2 stories with a dramatic opening | |||| | 5x |
| 22.4.00 | To include complex sentences in my next 3 stories | || | 2x |
| 19.6.00 | To begin information writing with a clear introduction | ||| | 3x |
| | | ||| | 3x |

*Fig. 5.5 Quantified writing targets*

# Wider issues

■ Informal, face-to-face target setting tends to take place before Year 1, often focusing on social targets (e.g. *'Let's see if by Friday your target can be to try not to get upset when your Mum says goodbye'*).

■ By Years 5 and 6, children are often set two targets, of contrasting nature, with longer to achieve them.

■ By Year 7, a natural development would be that children have the same system, but the discussion between teacher and child takes place via a marking dialogue (e.g. *'I notice you have done this aspect of your target twice now. How about trying to do…?'* etc. The child could then write to the teacher about his or her thoughts about help needed, for example.

# Writing the policy

Teachers on courses at the Institute of Education created a draft beginning to a target setting policy, which is shown on page 86. The next part of the strategy, where the school lists exactly what needs to happen to fulfil the principles, has to be created by each school.

---

**INSET ideas**

1. At an introductory staff meeting, give teachers copies of the 'child-speak' writing targets and the writing target prompt sheets (see Fig. 5.4 and website). Talk about the two systems and the importance of ipsative referencing. Ask different teachers to trial the two different systems over a term.

2. Give support by feedback meetings where teachers bring along examples of cards or flaps and talk about successes, problems and impact of the targets.

3. Ultimately, keep the targets under review by monitoring the cards or flaps to make sure they are being kept up to date. With child involvement as described, the children do not allow the targets to stop!

# TARGET SETTING POLICY

## Mission statement

Target setting in our school will involve all children and teaching staff in the identification and creation of achievable, challenging and measurable targets, based on previous achievement, aiming to raise self-esteem and fulfil learning potential.

## Principles

■ Targets should be at all levels: school, teacher, class, child.

■ Targets should be set as a result of analysis of available data.

■ Summative levels should be tracked at regular intervals and subsequent targets set.

■ The school achievement of national and local targets should result from individual targets.

■ Tracking of numerical targets should be linked to SEN provision, deployment of resources (all kinds), training needs, review of policies for external factors (e.g. attendance, travellers, lateness, welfare issues, EAZ provision).

■ Target setting should correspond to the school development plan in terms of focus, timing and funding.

■ Targets should be realistic, manageable and challenging.

■ Targets should be expressed in language which is accessible to all parties involved.

■ Targets should be shared with children in the short term and long term and with parents only in the long term.

■ Pupil participation is essential in the creation and meeting of targets.

■ Targets need to be reviewed and monitored by the LEA, governors, headteacher, curriculum coordinators and children (as appropriate to the type of target), and new targets set as a continual process.

■ Targets will be supported and met by effective teaching, learning and classroom assessment and strategies.

■ Target setting will be monitored, supported and reviewed as part of the school's monitoring policy.

# 6 Questioning

Teachers ask children many questions, many of which are closed, often unproductive. **Closed questions** imply that the teacher has a predetermined correct response in mind. These are nearly always concerned with the recall of facts or simple comprehension where the answer has previously been provided. **Open questions** allow for a range of responses and make progressive cognitive demands on children. They encourage children to think beyond the literal. The effective use of open, higher-order questions enables teachers to assist children's understanding and thinking.

Research on 'wait-time' showed that teachers need to leave five seconds after asking children a question, to allow them to respond. This is the optimum time it takes to process the question and formulate the answer. Most teachers, apparently, wait approximately two seconds before either asking another child or answering the question themselves. If this is the norm in a classroom, children often don't try to think of a response, because they know that the answer or another question will quickly follow. Children typically leave the answering of class questions to the few who appear to be able to respond quickly, and are unwilling to risk making mistakes in public. The teacher can keep a lesson going by questioning in this way, but ultimately knows that the understanding of only a few pupils has been revealed.

Black and Wiliam (1998) offer a few solutions:

> ■ *Give pupils time to respond: ask them to discuss their thinking in pairs or in small groups so that a respondent speaks on behalf of the others.*
>
> ■ *Give pupils a choice between different possible answers and ask them to vote on the options.*
>
> ■ *Ask all pupils to write down an answer and then read out a selected few.*

*What is essential is that any dialogue should evoke thoughtful reflection in which all pupils can be encouraged to take part.* **"**

The following strategies for effective questioning are taken from *Talking in Class*, a leaflet produced by the National Literacy Strategy. They are equally useful across all subjects.

**'**

**Invite pupils to elaborate**
Encourages pupils to develop more complex contributions.
*'Say a little more about...'*

**Echo**
Helps pupils clarify their own thinking, and shows they have been listened to.
*'So you think that...'*

**Non-verbal invitations**
Can signal to individuals to contribute or leave very open – a versatile response.
*Eye contact, tilt of head, nod, etc...*

**Make a personal contribution from your own experience**
Encourages pupils to offer contributions of their own, and see identification and empathy as useful tools.
*'I remember...'*

**Clarify ideas**
Makes the key points easier to grasp, and encourages children to consider viewpoints.
*'I can tell that is the case because...'*

**Make a suggestion**
Encourages pupils to offer their own suggestions or build on teacher's suggestion.
*'You could try...'*

**Reflect on topics**
Encourages pupils to explore the topic rather than seeking a single answer.
*'Yes, I sometimes think that...'*

**Offer information or make observation on a topic**
Encourages pupils to offer their own information and discuss the adult's contribution.
*'It might be useful to know that...'*

**Speculate on a given subject**
Encourages pupils to explore ideas, and understand that
uncertainty is a normal stage in the thinking process. **"**
(National Literacy Strategy, 1998)

Two aspects of questioning seem to be important:
questioning to elicit understanding during or after activities,
and the use of 'starting point' questions offered to children
as the essence of an activity. This chapter now takes
Numeracy, Literacy and Science in turn, focusing on
effective ongoing questioning as well as activity 'starting
point' questions.

# Questioning in the context of Mathematics

## During maths lessons

One of the reasons for children's fear of mathematics is that
it is very easy to get something wrong, and be told it is
wrong, without a chance to do anything about it. An
effective questioning strategy which enables children to
become more powerful in controlling their learning is to
simply repeat back their answer in a neutral tone, thereby
handing it back to them. The child will then either verify
the answer, or will be able to say whether they are sure or
not. In many cases, children look at their answer again in
response to this strategy and tell you the right answer. For
instance: *Teacher: 'So it's 42?'*, pause, then: *Child: 'Oh, no – it
can't be. I need to do it again.'*

This technique is also very effective when working with the
whole class. Let the mistake or wrong answer go on to the
flip chart or board and wait to see what happens. Invariably,
children spot the error. If we jump in to correct
immediately, children realise that they don't need to do any
active checking or thinking. Of course, the neutral stance
has to be maintained for right as well as wrong answers, or
children soon realise that it is only when answers are wrong
that it is handed back to them!

The National Numeracy Project publication *Mathematical
Vocabulary* shows the different kinds of questions possible
throughout a Numeracy lesson:

### Recalling facts
*What is 3 add 7?*
*How many days in a week?*

### Applying facts
*Tell me two numbers that have a difference of 12.*
*What unit would you use to measure the width of the table?*

### Hypothesising or predicting
*Estimate the number of marbles in this jar.*
*If we did our survey again on Friday, how likely is it that our graph would be the same?*

### Designing and comparing procedures
*How might we count this pile of sticks?*
*How could you subtract 37 from 82?*

### Interpreting results
*So what does that tell us about numbers that end in five or zero?*
*So what can we say about the sum of the angles in a triangle?*

### Applying reasoning
*The seven coins in my purse total 23p. What could they be?*
*Why is the sum of two odd numbers always even?*

*A range of questions to help extend children's thinking during mathematics lessons:*

### 1. Getting started
*What information do you have? What do you need to find out or do?*
*What equipment will you need?*
*What questions will you need to ask?*
*Can you predict the answer?*
*How are you going to record what you are doing?*

### 2. While children are working
*Can you explain what you have done so far?*
*What do you mean by...? What did you notice when...?*
*Why did you decide to use this method?*
*Do you think this would work with other numbers?*
*Are you beginning to see a pattern or a rule?*

### 3. Children who are stuck
*Can you describe the problem in your own words?*
*Could you talk me through what you have done so far?*
*Is there something that you already know that might work?*
*What about putting things in order?*
*Have you compared your work with anyone else?*

## 4. During the plenary

*How did you get your answer?*
*Can you describe your method to all of us? Can you explain why it works?*
*What could you try next?*
*What if you could only use...?*
*How did you check it?*

**"**

(*Mathematical Vocabulary*, National Numeracy Project)

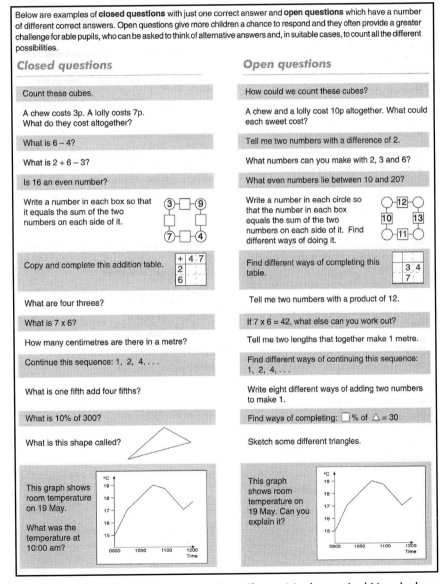

Below are examples of **closed questions** with just one correct answer and **open questions** which have a number of different correct answers. Open questions give more children a chance to respond and they often provide a greater challenge for able pupils, who can be asked to think of alternative answers and, in suitable cases, to count all the different possibilities.

| Closed questions | Open questions |
|---|---|
| Count these cubes. | How could we count these cubes? |
| A chew costs 3p. A lolly costs 7p. What do they cost altogether? | A chew and a lolly cost 10p altogether. What could each sweet cost? |
| What is 6 – 4? | Tell me two numbers with a difference of 2. |
| What is 2 + 6 – 3? | What numbers can you make with 2, 3 and 6? |
| Is 16 an even number? | What even numbers lie between 10 and 20? |
| Write a number in each box so that it equals the sum of the two numbers on each side of it. | Write a number in each circle so that the number in each box equals the sum of the two numbers on each side of it. Find different ways of doing it. |
| Copy and complete this addition table. | Find different ways of completing this table. |
| What are four threes? | Tell me two numbers with a product of 12. |
| What is 7 x 6? | If 7 x 6 = 42, what else can you work out? |
| How many centimetres are there in a metre? | Tell me two lengths that together make 1 metre. |
| Continue this sequence: 1, 2, 4, . . . | Find different ways of continuing this sequence: 1, 2, 4, . . . |
| What is one fifth add four fifths? | Write eight different ways of adding two numbers to make 1. |
| What is 10% of 300? | Find ways of completing: ☐ % of △ = 30 |
| What is this shape called? | Sketch some different triangles. |
| This graph shows room temperature on 19 May. What was the temperature at 10:00 am? | This graph shows room temperature on 19 May. Can you explain it? |

**Fig. 6.1 Closed and open questions** (from *Mathematical Vocabulary*, National Numeracy Project, Crown Copyright)

## *Questions as activities*

Many closed starting points can be converted to more open questions, where children will need to be involved in higher order thinking. *Mathematical Vocabulary* contains a useful chart illustrating examples of these (see Fig. 6.1).

# Questioning in the context of Literacy

Shaun Knight (2000), in the extremely useful booklet produced by Manchester School Improvement Service, lists different questioning strategies or techniques which can be used within the different parts of the Literacy Hour:

**Shared classwork – text level**
(N.B. Share learning objectives with pupils)

- *use questions to assess what pupils know;*

- *use a mixture of closed and open questions;*

- *use questions which go beyond recall in order to promote, challenge or broaden the range of experience of pupils;*

- *include as many pupils as possible;*

- *give pupils time to think before answering;*

- *target individuals, taking account of their attainment and needs;*

- *pursue a line of questioning with individual pupils to understand their thinking;*

- *ask questions in different ways so that pupils who do not understand first time may pick up the meaning subsequently;*

- *encourage pupils to ask each other questions.*

**Shared classwork – word/sentence level**

- *use questions to assess what pupils know or remember;*

- *ask pupils to demonstrate their thinking;*

*■ use questions to involve pupils as active participants, e.g. coming out to the board to write answers/underline, etc.*

### Guided groupwork – writing/reading

*Working with a small group offers the teacher greater opportunities to ask the pupils questions which enable them to reflect on their understanding and thinking. In time, this will engage them in a dialogue which will develop their critical thinking.*

*Through effective questioning, the teacher can assess the pupils' understanding and can move them forward in their learning.*

### Plenary

*■ use questions to summarise or emphasise key points for learning, linked to the learning objectives of the lesson;*

*■ listen to answers of explanations and use these in a positive way to demonstrate teaching points;*

*■ use questions to assess what pupils know and where common errors or misconceptions lie.* **,**

Knight divides questions used during literacy sessions into 'literal' (closed) and 'higher-order' (open). The following charts show the place, purpose and examples of the different kinds of questions, which should be useful for most aspects of the Literacy Hour. Statements written in italics are drawn from level descriptions, helping to identify and support progression.

## Literal questions

Literal questions all involve **recall**:

■ These questions are designed to help children recall or revise material which has already been covered.

■ They make relatively low intellectual demand on some children.

## Higher-order questions

Higher-order questions may be of four types: **application** questions, **analytical** questions, questions requiring **synthesis**, and **evaluation** questions.

| General examples of literal questions | Examples using the book *Cousteau: An Unauthorised Biography* |
| --- | --- |
| ■ Where does the story take place?<br><br>■ When did the story take place?<br><br>■ What did s/he/it look like?<br><br>■ Who was s/he/it?<br><br>■ Where did s/he/it live?<br><br>■ Who are the key characters in the book?<br><br>■ Where in the book would you find...? | ■ Who was Jacques Cousteau?<br><br>■ When was he born?<br><br>■ Where did he live?<br><br>■ What did he do in 1930? (look on back of book)<br><br>■ What did Cousteau and Emile Gagnan invent in 1943?<br><br>■ What major events happened in his life? |

## Application questions

■ Application means that the information learned can be applied in different contexts.

■ Children are able to transfer knowledge learned in one situation to another.

■ Children can make links with other stories.

| General examples of application questions | Examples using the book *Cousteau: An Unauthorised Biography* |
| --- | --- |
| ■ Can you think of another story which has a similar theme (e.g. good over evil, weak over strong, wise over foolish)?<br><br>■ Do you know another story which deals with the same issues (e.g. social, cultural, moral)?<br><br>■ Which other author handles time in this way (e.g. flashbacks, dreams)?<br><br>■ Which stories have openings like this? | ■ Do you know other texts with similar issues or themes?<br>E.g. *'Antarctic Journal'*<br>*'Viewpoints on Waste'*<br>*'Issues'*<br>*'Voices'* |

# Analytical questions

- This type of question requires the child to build on existing knowledge.

- They require the children to identify implicit meanings, make *inference and deduction* and become aware of the author's intentions.

- *They ask children to show an understanding of significant themes, ideas, events and characters and refer to the text when explaining views.*

| General examples of analytical questions | Examples using the book *Cousteau: An Unauthorised Biography* |
|---|---|
| ■ What makes you think that?<br><br>■ What words give you that impression?<br><br>■ How do you feel about…?<br><br>■ Can you explain why…?<br><br>■ Do you agree with …'s opinion?<br><br>■ I wonder what the writer intended?<br><br>■ I wonder why the writer has decided to…?<br><br>■ What was in the author's mind?<br><br>■ What do these words mean and why do you think the author chose them?<br><br>■ How has the author used adjectives to make this character funny?<br><br>■ Why did the author choose this setting?<br><br>■ Can you support your view with evidence?<br><br>■ Are there any familiar patterns you notice (e.g. familiar story structure, images, etc.)? | ■ What words give you the impression that Cousteau was a conservationist?<br><br>■ What is Cousteau's opinion about fishing?<br><br>■ How does the use of similes deepen our understanding and form or develop our opinions?<br><br>■ What kinds of animals are at risk?<br><br>■ Can you find evidence to support Cousteau's argument about mining?<br><br>■ In what context has Cousteau used the words 'key' and 'silent world' OR explain what Cousteau meant by 'silent world'. |

- These questions ask children to analyse mood, setting and characters, style, structure and other key aspects.
- They encourage children to *express opinions and preferences about major events or ideas in stories or poems.*
- *They ask children to refer to the text when explaining views.*

## Questions requiring synthesis

- These kinds of questions ask children to take an idea from one context and reapply it in another context.
- They encourage children to restructure text:

– rewriting a narrative as a diary;

– discussing a familiar story and changing elements;

– changing an explanatory text into a diagram.

- They ask children to innovate text (parody), e.g. *Alex and the Glass Slipper.*
- They ask children to develop a critical stance.
- *Children can retrieve and collate information from a range of sources.*
- This can lead to the construction of an argument or an opinion, or making predictions.

| General examples of questions requiring synthesis | Examples using the book *Cousteau: An Unauthorised Biography* |
|---|---|
| ■ What is your opinion? What evidence do you have to support your view?<br><br>■ Using all the evidence available, can you tell me what you feel about....?<br><br>■ Given what you know about...what do you think?<br><br>■ How would the views put across in these texts affect your views on...?<br><br>■ What would this character think about... (possibly a present-day issue)? | ■ If Cousteau were alive today, would he be arguing for environmentalists or the mining company? What evidence supports your view?<br><br>■ Think of a current environmental issue reported at the moment. What would Cousteau's view be?<br><br>■ What is your point of view? Can you support your view with evidence?<br><br>■ Given what you know about him, what are your views about Cousteau? |

■ *Children can select sentences, phrases and relevant information to support their views.*

## Evaluation questions

■ This type of question asks children to make judgements about what they have analysed and define the reasons for those judgements.

■ They also compare and contrast.

■ They interrogate and evaluate the story.

■ They require the use of evidence and reasoning.

| General examples of evaluation questions | Examples using the book *Cousteau: An Unauthorised Biography* |
|---|---|
| ■ What makes this a successful story? What evidence do you have to justify your opinion?<br>■ Does it work?<br>■ Could it be better? Is it as good as…?<br>■ Which is better, and why? | ■ Does Cousteau achieve what he set out to achieve?<br>■ Does he inspire you? Why?<br>■ Should diving be encouraged or is it responsible for harming the environment?<br>■ Cousteau thought that in the future people might live under the sea. If he was so concerned about conservation, why did he suggest that?<br>■ If Cousteau was so concerned about animals, why did he let one of his divers ride on the back of a whale? |

(Knight, 2000)

**References:** *Alex and the Glass Slipper* Magic Bean (ISBN 0-947212-96-5); *Antarctic Journal* Magic Bean (ISBN 1-86374-055-4); *Cousteau: An Unauthorised Biography* by Kevin Comber, Magic Bean in-fact (ISBN 0-947212-90-6); *Issues* Magic Bean (ISBN 0-947212-92-2); *Viewpoints on Waste* Magic Bean (ISBN 1-86374-052-X); *Voices* Magic Bean (ISBN 0-947212-59-0).

# Questioning in the context of Science

The work of Jos Elstgeest is used in this section, to illustrate possible strategies for planning a development of questions in science lessons. In his chapter, *'The right question at the right time'* (Elstgeest, 1985), he makes some useful points about questioning which can be applied to any subject:

1  Include the words *'do you think'* when asking a recall question. *'How many legs do you think an insect has?'* is more likely to elicit a response, than *'How many legs has an insect?'* because the child's answer will always be 'correct'.

2  Don't ask questions of this type until children have had the necessary experience they need so that they can reason from evidence.

3  Don't be afraid to say when you don't know the answer to something, or that nobody does.

4  When children ask 'Why?' questions, consider whether they have the experience to understand the answer.

5  Break up questions whose answers would be too complex into ones that concern relationships the children can find out about and understand.

Elstgeest explains how we often ask children open questions too soon in the process of an investigation. For instance, asking children *'Can you make a plant grow sideways?'* is likely to elicit a yes or no response, or a plethora of random ideas about how to set up this experiment. We need to structure the order of questioning in science so that children are fully conversant with the characteristics and properties of the subject of experimentation. They are then in a position to be able to design experiments. If children have found out as much as they can about what happens to plants in different circumstances, they will then be in a position to design a way to make it grow sideways.

I believe there is a parallel here with mathematics problem-solving. I can remember asking children to build the tallest tower possible with newspaper. I was disappointed that they spent so long pasting layers of newspaper together, when I wanted them to make tubes and strong constructions. In the end, I found myself giving them strategies to build the tower, so they really did very little 'problem-solving' themselves. I believe this is a common scenario in the classroom, with the teacher's questions often starting with *'Have you thought of…?'*. Elstgeest's order of questions is as follows:

1  Start with **attention-focusing** questions *(e.g. What can you see? What is this? What do you know about it?)*. This is the initial exploration stage.

2  Move on to **quantifying** questions *(e.g. How many? How long is it? How heavy is it?)*. Children find out more about the objects using measuring skills.

3  Lead in to **comparison** questions *(e.g. Is it longer than….? How much heavier is it than…..? In how many ways are your seeds alike and how do they differ?)*. Observations are sharper as a result of these questions. Children are naturally classifying and ordering their observations and data.

4  Suggest **action** questions *(e.g. What happens if you place your cress seeds in damp sand? …if you place a cutting or twig in water? …if you hold your magnet near a match?…)*. Children are encouraged to experiment and investigate relationships between what they do and the reaction of the thing they handle. *'What happens if'* questions should be preceded by an invitation to predict the outcome.

5  Children are now ready for **problem-posing** questions *(e.g. Can you find a way to make a plant grow sideways? …make a sinking object float? …separate salt from water?)*. Children have become familiar with the possibilities, impossibilities and properties of the objects under study. They are now capable of setting up for themselves hypotheses and situations to test them.

Elstgeest also points out, in a later article, that sometimes the logical procedure of a lesson does not work and might need to be turned on its head. For instance, he described one teacher trying to get her class to light up a bulb. She discovered that they had not yet developed even a rudimentary idea about closing a circuit. Elstgeest suggested that the teacher ask the question *'How many ways can you find to put the bulb out?'* and to get the children to draw it. The subsequent revived interest and new activity led to discussion about the drawings. This made the idea of closing and breaking a circuit begin to make full sense.

Further examples are:

> ■ *How would you stop a magnet from attracting a piece of iron?*
>
> ■ *How would you grow a plant without soil?*
>
> ■ *How could you drop an egg without breaking it?*
>
> ■ *Can you make a paper glider come back to you?*
>
> ■ *How would you keep ice from melting outside a freezer?*

(Elstgeest, 1992)

---

**INSET ideas**

1. Subject coordinators could lead staff meetings, sharing the contents of the relevant sections of this chapter. Teachers can be given specific activities to try in their classrooms for a feedback session.

2. Encourage teachers to practise some of the examples given in this chapter. The Literacy examples can be applied to a different book, with results reported back. Maths order of questions and some of the strategies for general maths questioning can be tried and reported back. Science lessons can be planned using the order of questions given, and reported back at a feedback meeting.

3. If helpful, an example book/maths activity or science starting point can be used by the whole staff during an INSET session, in groups creating the various types of questions using the examples given as a model. The discussion and the resulting questions will enrich teachers' repertoire of questioning skills generally and specifically.

# 7 Monitoring

Monitoring in schools is a key issue for ensuring consistency, continuity and that the rhetoric matches the reality. However, monitoring has associated time-management problems and, if set up inappropriately, can *determine* practice rather than monitor it. For example, it can be tempting to create paper systems that are easy to monitor, when they would be more effective if they were formatted differently. Getting the teaching and learning right should be the first priority, then how to monitor it the next.

This chapter covers two broad aspects of monitoring: *what* should be monitored and *how* it should be monitored. Of course, monitoring itself is of no use unless the monitoring information is used and followed up, improving or maintaining the current situation, so this will also be dealt with. Key features of this chapter will be elements of formative assessment.

## What should be monitored?

The core areas for monitoring are:

- **The curriculum**
  ensuring coverage, continuity and progression, use of resources, quality of learning.

- **Teaching**
  effectiveness in ensuring learning, classroom organisation, class control, etc.

- **Children's progress**
  day-to-day, year-on-year, equal opportunities.

- **Teacher development**
  identifying strengths and weaknesses and finding strategies for development (e.g. management, subject, general, personal).

The QCA (1999) document *Target Setting and Assessment in the National Literacy Strategy* included the following list, illustrating the various audiences of monitoring:

*The **class teacher** wants to know:*

- Has the class overall learned what I planned?

- Are all the children making progress?

- Are they making sufficient progress against national expectations?

- Which individuals need more help in which areas?

- Which children need extension work?

- Is my planning for activities, resources and staffing well targeted?

- How can I do it better next time?

*The **headteacher and other teachers** want to know:*

- Are the children making progress?

- Are there any major problems?

- How does their performance compare with those in parallel classes or in other years?

- Is the children's progress in line with the school's targets?

- How is the school doing in comparison with other schools?

- What aspects of our curriculum and teaching need to be strengthened?

*The **parents/carers** want to know:*

- Is my child making good progress?

- Are there any major problems?

- How is my child doing compared with others of the same age?

- What can I do to help?

*The **LEA and national government** want to know:*

- How is the school and LEA progressing against their targets?

■ Are the school development plans working?

■ What national curriculum levels are children achieving in teacher assessment and tests at ages seven and eleven?

■ How is the school doing in comparison with other similar schools?

■ Are the priorities of the LEA's Education Development Plan being met? **'**

I would like to add another element to this list: the child.

*The **child** wants to know:*

■ Am I making appropriate progress?

■ Is there anything I need to do to improve my progress?

■ Are my individual needs being catered for?

■ Is my work planned so that it is just right for me – not too easy or too difficult, despite the needs of the curriculum and statutory tests?

■ Do I get an appropriate balance of subjects?

■ Do I get the chance to use different learning styles?

■ Do I have a chance to be self-evaluative and have those thoughts been taken account of?

# How should monitoring take place?

A good starting-point is to consider the possible monitoring mechanisms. These form a menu, which establishes the backbone of a monitoring framework. We then need to consider the various advantages and disadvantages of each mechanism and decide which are most effective.

## *Possible monitoring mechanisms*

### Formal strategies (time needed)

1. Work sampling/taking in all books/taking samples at random

2. Classroom observations

3. Headteacher (HT)/Year group termly monitoring of planning + work + target card samples

4. Classroom observations + work sampling + target sampling

5. Job profiling/teacher appraisal/performance management

6. Discussion between HT and Curriculum Coordinator (CC)

7. Discussion between HT and class teacher

8. Discussion between CC and class teacher

9. Analysis of test data

10. Tracking of numerical targets

11. Analysis of LEA comparative data

12. Analysis of national comparative data

13. Analysis of medium-term plans

14. Analysis of short-term plans

15. Analysis of school reports

16. Analysis of actual pupil writing/maths targets

17. Analysis of IEP targets

18. Looking through children's work

19. CC checking use of resources throughout school

20. HT checking effective use of people as resources

21. Playtime observations

## Informal, incidental or externally based strategies

22. Headteacher training

23. Observation of sharing assemblies

24. Pupil feedback

25. Parent feedback

26. Governor feedback

27. Staff meeting feedback

28. Informal exchanges (before and after school, etc.)

29. SENCO perspective

30. External perspective (e.g. inspectors)

In deciding on regular formal monitoring mechanisms, it is important to select strategies which are most time-effective. Teachers tend to find that it is more effective to have a longer, richer, less frequent monitoring time than to have many discrete monitoring activities taking place across the school. For example, taking in samples of children's work across a year group or school for scrutiny by curriculum coordinators is often a superficial exercise. Without the teacher present, and the corresponding weekly plan, sampled work can have too many missing factors for any worthwhile or rigorous judgement to be made. *Combining* monitoring mechanisms (see nos. 3 and 4 above) makes monitoring more satisfying and effective, because the links can be made between planning, subsequent learning, work products and targets. These combined monitoring strategies are now described in full.

## No. 3. Headteacher/Year group termly monitoring of planning + work sampling + target card samples

Many heads still insist that short-term plans (weekly plans which show each day's lessons) are passed to the head on a Monday morning. This can create work for the head and result in very little impact on teaching. Giving in plans ensures that teachers do the planning in the first place. The same can be achieved, if it is still an issue in a school, by asking teachers to display their short-term plans on the classroom wall on a Monday morning for children and all adults involved with the class to see. (It is important to make the point that the way this plan looks on Monday will be different to how it will look on Friday, when assessment jottings, crossings out and various scribbled notes have turned it into a messy and dynamic document.) Then the monitoring of planning can be considered more carefully.

More and more schools now ask for plans to be taken in only now and again, often on a Friday rather than a Monday. This means that the head can focus on assessment notes and the changes made, rather than a hypothetical plan which has not yet been used. If plans are taken in this way, it is a good idea for the head to have a specific monitoring focus, for a half-term period. For instance, focusing on the match between learning intentions and tasks, or the quality of assessment jottings and whether they really are about informing future planning, or take two consecutive plans in at a time and see whether there is evidence of the assessment jottings being taken account of in the second plan. If this is followed up by feedback to the staff at a staff meeting, or to individuals if necessary, *action* is then a direct result of the monitoring activity. Without subsequent action, monitoring is not useful.

A termly planning meeting between deputy/head/Literacy and Numeracy coordinators and each year group in turn, during lunch hours or after school, can enable teachers to have face-to-face dialogue about their planning. Next term's medium-term planning and all the short-term plans for the term so far would be brought to the meeting. If work samples and writing target cards are also brought along to this meeting, these can be discussed in context, with full information (i.e. cross-referencing to lesson plans, etc.) allowing judgements about progress and consistency to be made more accurately. The person leading the meeting might say *'Let's all look at week 3's science lesson. Let's go round now and look at the match between the learning intention and the actual content of the lesson. Then we'll look at the work you've brought along from that lesson.'* Although this time needs to be found in the first place, time is released from other monitoring activities, such as analysing work samples, talking to teachers in turn or spending hours poring over plans away from teachers.

## No. 4. Classroom observations + work sampling + target sampling

Lesson observations can also be the vehicle for looking at samples of work and writing targets, again made more meaningful when set in the context of the live lesson. Classroom observations are a regular feature of most schools now, with various adults in the schools involved in this form of monitoring, so the issues around observations need a closer focus.

# Classroom observations up close

Classroom observations can be carried out by the following people, with the following possible focuses:

| | |
|---|---|
| **Head or deputy** | A current focus, often linked with school development plan or current initiatives or school targets: e.g. foundation subjects, classroom organisation, literacy, numeracy, teaching skills, general quality of learning. |
| **Curriculum coordinators** | For their subject: adequate and effective use of resources, appropriate subject coverage and knowledge, learning matched to intentions. |
| **Class teachers (peer observations)** | Individual subject need, general effectiveness of teaching and learning. |

## Conditions for successful observation

In order to make classroom observations manageable and worthwhile, we need to look at conditions for success, how time can be found and how observations can be followed up. The following lists are drawn from research about monitoring as well as feedback from heads and teachers.

■ There needs to be a whole-school policy and structure for observations.

■ Ideally the School Development Plan should suggest the focus for observation.

■ Planning needs to be clear and tight to enable monitoring to have a starting point (i.e. what is the learning intention and the matched activity?).

■ Observer and teacher need to agree the focus, terms and nature of what is to be observed.

■ Only key points should be recorded by the observer.

■ Short feedback should follow on the same day.

■ Observer should first ask the teacher how the session went.

■ Observer should sum up discussion and offer suggestions.

■ Both should keep a copy of the final summary and action, for follow-up use.

Of key importance when carrying out classroom observations is that the criteria for observation are written and given to the person being observed, so that both observer and observee are aware of the aspects being judged. Without this knowledge, the teacher is cast in the role of the child who does not know the learning intention of a task. Too many criteria can make the observer spend the entire time trying to keep track of them and much of a lesson can be missed by the observer writing furiously. It is better to have a few focused criteria. Whatever the subject of the person observing, formative assessment will be embedded in the practice of a school if there are always some generic assessment criteria listed for observations.

The following list simply turns the various formative assessment strategies into observation criteria:

## Generic assessment criteria for observations

■ Is the learning intention clearly shown in the short-term plan?

■ s there a match between learning intention and task?

■ Is the learning intention shared explicitly with children, both orally and visually, at the beginning of the session?

■ Is the learning intention the focus of oral feedback and/or written marking during the session?

■ Is there some opportunity for children to reflect against the learning intention of the session using self-evaluation?

## How are observations followed up?

■ Feed back to teacher at once, using a simple proforma to record action.

■ Follow up at next observation.

■ Follow up at job profiling/appraisal meeting.

■ Pick up in HT/Year group termly monitoring of planning meetings.

If teachers feel threatened by classroom observations, the following aspects can help build a monitoring culture. However, monitoring will only be considered worthwhile by teachers if they can see the positive effects and follow-up for the children and/or the school, or in their own personal development.

## Creating an observation/monitoring culture

■ Make observation commonplace:

– Headteacher monitoring first;

– Getting inspectors to observe;

– Organise pairs of teachers to observe other schools.

■ Introduce job profiling, which links with observations.

■ Ensure observation rules are established, especially the focus and criteria.

■ Ensure that subject coordinators are sufficiently expert to be able to give advice.

■ Ensure teaching is underpinned by effective planning procedures.

| Who | What | How |
|---|---|---|
| **Head/Deputy** | Effectiveness of teaching | Analysis of LEA comparative data, classroom observations, tracking of individual numerical targets |
| | Effectiveness of learning | Work sampling, looking through work, pupil feedback, analysis of test data, analysis of actual writing/maths targets, classroom observations, analysis of IEP targets |
| | Effectiveness of getting high SAT scores | Analysis of test data and projected and actual individual targets |
| | School's progress in LEA | Analysis of LEA comparative data, external perspective |
| | School's progress in national context | Analysis of national comparative data |
| | Effectiveness of School Development Plan | Staff meeting feedback, discussion between Head and Curriculum Coordinators |
| | Ethos, behaviour, attitudes | Head teaching, observation of sharing assemblies, pupil feedback, parent feedback, classroom observations, SENCO perspective, staff meetings, playtime observations |
| | Support for colleagues by Curriculum Coordinators | Staff meeting feedback, informal exchanges, job profiling/performance management |
| | Development and impact of Curriculum Coordinators' work in meeting curriculum targets | Job profiling, discussion between HT and class teacher, tracking children's numerical targets, external perspective (if regular) |
| **Curriculum coordinators** | Continuity, consistency and progression | Discussion between HT and CC, overview of long- and medium-term plans/schemes of work, classroom observations, taking in all books or selecting random samples |
| | Adequate and effective use of resources | HT teaching, analysis of medium-term plans/schemes of work, classroom observations, HT checking use of people resources, CC checking resource use in school |
| | Appropriate subject coverage and knowledge throughout school | Analysis of medium-term plans, classroom observations, discussions between CC and class teacher |
| **Class teachers** | Children's day-to-day progress | Analysis of actual writing targets, analysis of short-term plans, informal exchanges, looking through children's work |
| | Addressing learning needs through planning | Analysis of short-term plans |
| | Individual children's overall (summative) progress | Tracking of numerical targets, analysis of school reports, SENCO perspective, looking at children's work |

*Fig. 7.1 A monitoring framework*

# Creating a school policy for monitoring

## *A monitoring framework*

After deciding *what* should be monitored and the virtues of different kinds of monitoring strategies, the next step is to link the two together. The framework in Fig. 7.1 is useful for linking the monitoring mechanisms (see pages 103-5) to what is to be monitored (see page 101). Of course, all the strategies could be linked with *every* aspect, so a good way to complete the chart is to decide what strategy *must* be used in the first instance (e.g. learning cannot be monitored without classroom observations).

The next step is to devise a monitoring calendar, which slots the strategies into regular times. This needs to be organised in months or half-terms and displayed so that all staff are aware of the ongoing monitoring schedule.

Alternatively, any chart which shows what, who, when and other vital information will be helpful in establishing monitoring routines. Fig. 7.2 shows some possibilities.

As well as the monitoring schedule and examples of observation criteria and so on, the written policy for monitoring needs to include – as in all policies – key aims and principles. The following policy is the result of one infant school's focus on monitoring.

---

## MONITORING AND EVALUATION POLICY

*May 2000*                                                            *Review 2003*

### Aims

We aim for all children to have the best opportunities for high achievement through an accessible and relevant curriculum. A planned approach to monitoring and evaluation of teaching and the curriculum enables the school to:

■ Find out about the quality of teaching and learning and the standards of achievement.

# Fig. 7.2 Monitoring schedules

**Monitoring Activities**

Annually

- Formal review of the School Development Plan in the Spring term involving whole staff, governors, parents and children.
- Moderation of the SATs in Year 2.
- Target setting and SATs data.
- Using the Panda and other benchmark data.
- Curriculum policies as indicated on the SDP.
- Moderation in core areas.
- Performance management reviews.

Termly

- Target setting and review. (Spring/summer term).
- Termly curriculum plans.
- Samples of work in maths and english for the pupil profile.
- Review of Action Plan.
- Analysis of class reading record.
- SEN reviews.
- Work samples over time in the core areas (for the ROLO).
- Baseline assessment (twice yearly).

Other

**Monitoring Overview**

| Autumn | Method/Focus | By Whom |
|---|---|---|
| Classroom observation   Y1  Y2 | Work sampling + obs T+L/ethos/progress | HT |
| Monitoring IEPs | SENCO LAs  CTs monitor progress/progress   1day each class | EH |
| Analysis of National/LEA/School SAT results | Comparative analysis | HT DH |
| Analysis of Baseline assessment | Comparative analysis + inform planning and ind. pupil targets | RW PW |
| Governor monitoring | Obs. visit by govs.focus agreed with co-ords linked to SDP | Link gov |
| Health and Safety monitoring | H+S Gov monitoring visit complete audit with HT | Gov HT |
| School Development Adviser visit | Obs. discussion focus linked to SDP and LEA/DfEE initiatives | AF |
| Planning and forecast meeting | HT+Yr group Ts analyse med and sh term plans | HT Ts |
| Co-ordinator monitoring | Prioritised by SDP class obs/work sampling/med+s t planning | Co-ords |

| Spring | | |
|---|---|---|
| Classroom observation   YR  Y2 | Work sampling + obs T+L/ethos/progress | HT |
| Monitoring IEPs | SENCO LAs  CTs monitor progress/progress   1day each class | EH |
| Analysis of Baseline assessment | Comparative analysis | RW PW |
| Governor monitoring | Comparative analysis + inform planning and ind. pupil targets | Link gov |
| School Development Adviser visit | Obs. visit by govs.focus agreed with co-ords linked to SDP | AF |
| Planning and forecast meeting | HT+Yr group Ts analyse med and sh term plans+pupils work>JPs | HT Ts |
| Analysis of class targets Y1 Y2 | SENCO and class Yr 1 Ts analyse MIST inform planning and target setting | Co-ords |
| Analysis of Middle Infant Screening | Prioritised by SDP class obs/work sampling/med+s t planning | |
| Co-ordinator monitoring | | |

| Summer | | |
|---|---|---|
| Classroom observation   YR  Y1 | Work sampling + obs T+L/ethos/progress | HT |
| Monitoring IEPs | SENCO LAs  CTs monitor progress/progress   1day each class | EH  Ts |
| Governor monitoring | Obs. visit by govs. focus agreed with co-ords linked to SDP | Co-ords |
| School Development Adviser visit | HT+Yr group focus linked to SDP and LEA/DfEE initiatives | |
| Planning and forecast meeting | Track ind pupil progress against prev targets plans+p | |
| Analysis of class targets Y1 Y2 YR | Prioritised by SDP class obs/work | |
| SATs analysis | | |
| Co-ordinator monitoring | | |

Ongoing – Teacher monitoring of pupil progress

| MONITORING PROGRAMME / TYPE OF MONITORING | WHO BY? | WHEN? | HOW RECORDED? | REPORTED TO? |
|---|---|---|---|---|
| Strategic Information Service | Headteacher + SCC | annually | SIS form and report | Governors, staff |
| Value Added project | Headteacher + SCC | annually | Value added report | Governors, staff |
| Analysis SATs | Headteacher, Y2 & Y6 teachers | summer | County tables, school statistics, pupils records, school prospectus. | Parents, Governors, staff |
| Analysis Y4 NC assessments | Headteacher, Y4 teachers | summer | School statistics, pupils records. | Parents, governors, staff |
| Analysis Y3 screening | Headteacher, Y3 teachers | autumn | County statistics, school statistics, pupils records | Parents, staff |
| Analysis N & R screening | Headteacher, EY teachers | autumn | County statistics, school statistics, pupils records. | Parents, governors, staff |
| Analysis Reading progress tests* | Headteacher, Language CC, infant & junior class teachers | summer | School statistics, pupils records. | Parents, staff |
| Assessment for SEN | EP, LSS, medical authority | as required | EP/LSS/medical records, pupil's SEN records | Parents, HT, SENCo, relevant staff |
| Internal individual support assessments | SENCo, SNAs, class teachers | as required | Pupil's SEN records | Parents if IEP, SENCo, relevant staff |
| Examining planning | Headteacher, Curriculum co-ordinators | annually | Monitoring file | Classteachers |
| Examining reports | Headteacher | annually | Monitoring file | Curriculum Co-ordinators |
| SEN days | SENCo, Headteacher | once a term | SEN records, IEPs | Parents if IEP, relevant staff |
| Teacher interviews | Headteacher, Curriculum co-ordinators | once a term + as required | Job profiles, monitoring files | classteacher |
| Classroom observation | Headteacher, Curriculum co-ordinators | bi-annually | monitoring files | classteacher |
| Work sampling | Headteacher, Curriculum co-ordinators | annually | monitoring files | governors via HT report and visiting governor reports |
| Observation of work (displays, assemblies etc) | Headteacher, Curriculum co-ordinators, governors | constant | monitoring file | child |
| Classroom assessment procedures | Classteacher | constant | Teachers' markbook, Teachers' notebook, short term planning, child's record, child's book. | child |
| Assessing / marking work produced | Classteacher | constant | Teachers' markbook, Teachers' notebook, short term planning, child's record, child's book. | child |
| Day to day assessment | Classteacher, classroom assistant, special needs assistant. | Constant | Teachers' notebook, short term planning, CA/SNAs records child's record, child's book. | |

*New initiative introduced Nov 1997

- Identify strengths and weaknesses.
- Identify areas for development and to take appropriate action.
- Ensure consistency in continuity and progression.
- Provide appropriate support and resources.
- Ensure the needs of all groups of children are addressed.
- Share good practice.

### Equal opportunities

Equal opportunities are central to our work and through monitoring and evaluation we are intent on identifying trends and patterns in achievement that may prevent all groups from making progress. When assessing the curriculum particular attention is given to discussing data arising from statutory testing (SATs, baseline, school records) with particular reference to gender issues, ethnicity, special needs, summer born, free school meals and attendance.

### The monitoring process

**Why?** The purpose of the activity is to gather information and may be linked to the School Development Plan and Action Plans. A monitoring activity could take place at the request of a teacher who may wish for support in developing an area.

**What?** The specific focus should be manageable for example, an aspect of a policy or scheme of work, a particular aspect of teaching, analysing SATs information or reviewing documentation.

**Who?** Personnel involved could include any of the following: teachers, support staff, parents and governors.

**How?** Monitoring should take second place to learning needs. Systems should first meet learning and teaching needs and then the question of how monitoring will take place needs to be considered, not the other way round. Methodology for monitoring could include looking at documents such as policies and schemes of work, baseline assessment, SATs, records, sampling of children's work, discussion with teachers and children, observation in the classroom, reviewing provision of resources, analysis of teacher planning and assessment.

### What is monitored?

*The curriculum*

- Coverage, continuity and progression
- Use of resources
- Quality of Learning.

*Teaching*

■ Effectiveness in ensuring learning

■ Classroom organisation

■ Class control

■ Ethos.

*Children's progress*

■ Day to day

■ Year to year

■ Equal opportunities.

*Teacher development*

■ Identifying strengths and weaknesses, and finding strategies for development for example, management, subject, general and personal.

*Anything else that needs checking!*

**Personnel involved**

The Head and all teaching staff and governors are involved in monitoring and evaluation.

■ The Curriculum Coordinator monitors medium-term planning throughout the school for their own subject(s).

■ The Headteacher monitors standards of teaching and learning by monitoring and reporting on benchmarking, standardised assessments, observing teaching, looking at children's work (including previous work, work produced during the lesson and work on display).

■ The Curriculum Coordinator monitors standards of teaching and learning mainly by looking at children's work and by talking to teachers. They collect samples, look at displays and look at work produced by staff in moderation sessions and by observing sharing and class assemblies. Limited classroom observation takes place together with advising other members of staff possibly during release time.

■ The Curriculum Coordinator manages resources including maintenance, storage and replacement within the confines of the allocated budget.

■ The Headteacher monitors finance.

■ The Headteacher and curriculum leaders keep records of all monitoring undertaken. As a minimum these notes include the date, the activity, the area and class and any observations.

■ Teachers monitor children's ongoing progress through target setting and through assessment.

■ Monitoring by the SENCO is covered in the Special Needs Policy.

**Current procedures**

■ The School Development Plan is reviewed annually in the Spring Term to discuss progress and identify issues for the following year.

■ The Senior Management Team meet weekly to review aspects of the School Development Plan.

■ The Literacy and Numeracy coordinators, ICT coordinator and SENCO meet with the SMT termly to discuss progress towards meeting targets on curriculum action plans.

■ Curriculum Coordinators monitor planning to ensure continuity and progression. They audit resources, sample work and lead policy review. Samples and records are kept in their coordinators' file.

■ The Head carries out a curriculum overview each half term and in this way curriculum content and progression is monitored.

■ The SENCO monitors individual and group IEPs together with the work of the Learning Support Assistants.

■ In the Autumn term reception teachers complete an analysis of baseline assessment. This is reviewed in the Spring term.

■ Governors monitor the work of the school through visits. Their focus is agreed with coordinators and is linked to the School Development Plan.

■ An LEA representative, the School Development Adviser, monitors school improvement on a termly basis.

■ A detailed SATs analysis takes place in the Summer term. SATs results are compared with targets previously set. All teachers are involved in this process but the responsibility is with the Year 2 staff.

■ The Head and Deputy meet each month to discuss issues arising from formal and informal monitoring activities.

■ Ongoing school evaluation using OFSTED criteria and the Essex Quality Framework.

**Evaluation and feedback**

Following an evaluation of the outcomes of the monitoring exercise areas of strengths and weaknesses are identified and any area for intervention or action is highlighted.

The monitoring process is normally discussed at the Senior Management Team weekly meeting and feedback to staff normally takes place at the regular weekly staff meetings where areas are discussed and appropriate action is agreed.

**Action and intervention**

This can include support for staff, provision for resources, further monitoring, provision of INSET courses, revision of policy or practice, sharing of good practice and ideas, revision of action plans and School Development Plan.

**Timing**

A timetable for monitoring which includes specific activities that happen on a termly or annual basis is included in the appendix.

Ongoing pupil monitoring by teaching and support staff takes place on a day-to-day basis, often as part of the planning process.

Subject curriculum monitoring takes places in staff meetings, at the end of the school day and during timetabled non-contact time. The frequency of curriculm monitoring is indicated on the School Development Plan.

**Reviewing the monitoring process**

These questions help to review the implementation of the monitoring policy.

■ Do the activities take place?

■ Are coordinators becoming more involved in monitoring activities?

■ Has INSET been planned to help them in this role?

■ Is there adequate time available for this to take place?

■ Are there any particular trends and patterns emerging from statistical analysis?

■ Is there consistency in planning and record keeping?

■ Are our expectations of achievement clear?

■ Are standards and achievement improving for all groups of children?

This policy will be reviewed in 2003.

**INSET ideas**

1.  Audit the school's current monitoring practice, determining the effectiveness of the monitoring strategies in action so far.

2.  Introduce the monitoring strategies list and the framework chart at a staff meeting and ask teachers in year groups or other groups to slot the numbers onto the chart. The discussion needed to do this will get everyone thinking about what is really useful in monitoring the different aspects.

3.  Away from the meeting, senior managers compare the charts and come up with a draft framework for the year.

4.  The various elements of monitoring need to be finely tuned. For example, creating simple proformas for observations and criteria lists for classroom observations.

5.  Have a staff meeting after the first year to review the effectiveness of the monitoring strategies used in the school's programme of monitoring.

6.  Continue the process of review.

# 8 Raising children's self-esteem

As stated throughout this book, and backed up by a wealth of research, the extent of children's self-esteem is the key to their learning success. Indeed, one could say the same for teachers. Major findings about self-esteem form the heart of this chapter.

A central theme is that we need to be more explicit in the language we use in the classroom, and think more carefully in our schools about strategies to raise children's self-esteem. A school which builds self-esteem via rewards, praise and sanctions is paying lip service to self-esteem, contributing to a culture in which self-esteem increases most for those children who already have a high self-esteem and where self-esteem 'rewards' are inevitably applied unevenly.

## Perceptions of learning and ability

Ask yourself to think of a subject which you believe you are good at. Now think of a subject at which you believe you are not so good. Which was easier? For the majority of teachers, and I believe for adults generally, our perceived failings feature more readily in our thoughts than our perceived successes. Much of this is established at an early age by relatively trivial means, such as an insensitive teacher or parent reinforcing for us that we are 'no good' at a particular subject. Various researchers (e.g. Vispoel and Austin, 1995) urge teachers to talk to children about the nature of learning: that learning is a continuum on which we are all placed and that, *given enough time and input*, anyone can master. This is not to say that we can all be Mozart or Einstein, but that, given enough time and input, we could all match the subject we think we are worst at to the level of the subject we think we are the best at. Motivation is of course assumed, once you know that the development is possible.

Dweck (1986) described the difference between positive and negative approaches to learning. She found that **positive** attitudes exist when children:

■ believe that effort leads to success;

■ accept that they have the ability to improve and learn;

■ prefer and feel satisfied on completing challenging tasks.

**Negative** attitudes, on the other hand, are manifested when children:

■ believe that success is related to ability;

■ enjoy doing better than others;

■ evaluate themselves negatively when the task is too difficult.

One of the problems about perceived ability is that it tends to be linked with learning *rate*. Once children or adults see someone in their peer group apparently grasping something more quickly, the assumption is made that they must have greater ability. Yet we have all known cases of early burn-out or late developers or people who have a faster rate of learning in one subject compared to another. Within a given subject, a number of factors determine learning aptitude – such as preferred learning and thinking style, personal circumstances for that day, previous experience of the subject matter, genetic disposition, relationship with the teacher, opportunities for self-evaluation and use of rewards, as well as physical wellbeing and comfort.

Much recent work on brain research, as well as Howard Gardner's famous 'multiple intelligences' and Daniel Goleman's 'emotional intelligence' have alerted educators to the multi-faceted and changing understanding and nature of ability or intelligence. This means we cannot have simple, one-track solutions for effective learning, as different learners need different modes of learning, and all learners can choose the way they think and learn. In fact, we cannot be sure any more of what ability or intelligence really amounts to. What is essential is that the classroom and school culture is embedded with the belief that *all* children *can* learn, something not widely associated with teacher beliefs in England. The common view is that there is a range of ability in a classroom, with some learning a lot and others learning very little.

## The melting pot of achievement

Various research has indicated that children who achieve significantly in non-academic subjects often have increased success in more academic subject areas. There is, in other words, a 'knock-on' effect from one achievement to another. We need to be capitalising on this effect by enabling children to see that achievements lead to further achievements, because of the related rise in confidence and self-esteem. Unfortunately, we tend to constrain children to subject tunnel vision, so that they believe that success in sport, for instance, will only lead to more success in sport. We need to tell children, explicitly, that an achievement in sport will now lead to improvement in, say, reading and vice versa. As adults, we know that confidence is gained whatever the achievement, making us have a greater sense of self-efficacy (the feeling of power to do something) for the next, perhaps unrelated task we tackle. Schools do not tend to make clear this 'melting pot' effect.

# External rewards: a sticky issue

One of the most controversial aspects of self-esteem is the use of rewards in schools. Many schools are now flooded with cartoon celebration stickers, smiley faces and the like, as well as team points, gold cards and various other schemes. OFSTED asks how achievement is being rewarded in a school and this seems to have been taken completely literally. Also, commercial companies inundate schools with free rolls of stickers at every opportunity. External rewards might be enjoyed by children, but research shows that they do not promote a 'learning culture' (Lepper and Hodell, 1989). **Children are encouraged to strive for the reward rather than for the achievement.**

A negative by-product of external rewards is that they have the same effect as grades or effort remarks: children focus on ego-involved attributions and comparison with peers ('I'm

*better than you', 'How many smiley faces have you got?').*
Teachers claim that they give external rewards fairly and for
a range of good work and deeds, but in various studies
where external rewards have been tracked, it always emerges
that three groups of children receive them more than
others: *children with special needs, brighter children* and
*naughty children.* Ignored every time is the middle section of
the class, those 'invisible', self-contained children who work
solidly and cause no behavioural problems.

What we are dealing with here is a situation where teachers
tend to focus on the smiling face of the child who receives
the reward, rather than looking at the face of the child who
does not. However, because children who don't get the
rewards tend to be less obvious, they often do not show
what they are thinking or feeling. If they made a fuss, the
teacher would look for a way of giving them an external
reward! These children know they are being ignored and, in
most cases, attribute it to lack of ability. I have had much
anecdotal evidence from parents whose children go home
delighted with their efforts in a poem or story, saying that
they are sure their teacher will be pleased with it, then come
home the following day saying *'I didn't get a sticker'.* If the
focus is the *learning*, then children receive feedback, as
described in Chapter 4, about their successes and
improvement needs against the learning intention, so every
child is task-focused, rather than ego-focused. An external
reward reduces the feedback to a tick or a cross – you've
made it or you haven't – and freezes children into inaction.
Improvement seems unnecessary if you have a reward, and
unattainable if you haven't.

There is a parallel with the allocation of grades in secondary
schools. In marking children's work with grades
(competitive task orientation), teachers can be said to have
focused children continually on the level of their ability
compared to their peers. With a focus on feedback against
the learning intentions of the *task*, however, children are
enabled to improve realistically against past performance. It
is important, of course, to know how one's performance
compares with one's peers or against set criteria, but when
this is the feedback for *every* piece of work, complacency or
demoralisation sets in (Butler, 1988), thus impeding
progress.

External rewards cannot be removed overnight. Children will think they have all been naughty! Teachers' feedback shows that the 'learning culture' of a school needs to be developed first, using the strategies outlined in this book: sharing learning intentions, pupil self-evaluation, and giving feedback against the learning intention, all in an explicit way. By this time, most teachers find they are feeling uncomfortable with the external rewards. If all children have three highlights for success, who should receive the stickers? When children receive appropriate feedback, reward schemes appear to be inadequate and patronising. Parents, governors and children all need to be told that, over time, these rewards are being phased out, citing the research evidence and showing what will happen instead. In schools where external rewards do not exist, the language of achievement is ritualised to become the reward. For instance:

> *Anna – you have just written your first sentence! What have you done?*

> *I've written my first sentence.*

> *That is wonderful. Would you like to take it now to the head and show her? Tell her what you can now do. What will you say to your Mum tonight?*

When children receive certificates or stickers, their description of their achievement is couched in terms of the reward: *'I got a sticker!'* The reward supersedes the achievement.

I believe there is a relationship between external rewards systems and the level of success of a school. No highly successful school I have come across, in a range of areas, uses external rewards. The head of such a school explained it to me in this way:

*'We won't patronise our children by putting cartoons on their work and giving them tokenistic symbols. When we first stopped external rewards the parents used to ask about it, but now it is established as the ethos of the school. We make a point of saying, when showing new parents around the school, that we are not that kind of school. We are more confident now about saying what we do and what we don't do.'*

(Anna House, Ridgeway Primary School, Croydon)

Another wrote to me about the shift from extrinsic to intrinsic rewards in her school, using formative assessment strategies as a framework:

*'The philosophy fits in well with our ethos, which is very positive and built upon trust, respect and fruitful interaction between all members of the community. We try to foster pride in our school and make an effort to quietly commend and celebrate achievement in appropriate ways. We have identified times at the beginning and the end of each school term for induction purposes, and it is at these times that values and rewards are discussed in order to promote the common view. We do talk with the children about them being in control of what happens to them rather than being victims of an adult-imposed regime. When they feel in control of their own learning, or their own behaviour, and they are made aware of the consequences of successful learning, or appropriate actions, and this is given a high profile by everyone, then the ball starts to roll and to gain momentum.'*

(Jenny Short, Lodden Junior School, Earley)

A good starting point is to ask Year 5 and 6 children to write their personal feelings about the current reward systems in the school. It is difficult for children to be open and honest in a class discussion, so writing works best. Of course, this has to be presented to children in a neutral way, or they will say what they think you want them to say. Something like *'We are not sure whether the rewards we use in the school really help you or not, or make you feel good or not, when you do or don't receive one. We want to know what you think. Are they fair? Are they a good thing? Are they necessary?'* etc. Teachers who have done this find that the children's comments reflect the research findings.

The following written comments from a Year 6 class about rewards would be a good basis for discussion with staff. Analyse the following statements – what do the children's comments say about how children of different abilities are rewarded, about their perceptions of their ability, about the feedback the reward gives them and what matters in school?

## About stickers...

*'I like having stickers – I have been noticed, but when I try hard and I don't get one I get disappointed.'* (middle ability)

*'Some people just do something just to get a sticker and soon they forget what they understood.'* (lower ability)

*'Stickers mean I get something right.'* (middle ability)

*'I don't think stickers actually do anything – comments from your teacher are better.'* (upper ability)

*'Stickers don't work the same in each classroom – so you work towards them one year and the following years no stickers, so no goals.'* (upper ability)

# About certificates...

*'I like notes you get in books – because you get them at the bottom of your work. Certificates you only get now and again.'* (upper ability)

*'In four years I've collected three certificates, so I don't bother about them.'* (middle ability)

*'I've only got one – they're not all that important to me.'* (middle ability)

*'When I got my certificate I achieved my goal, so I didn't continue to work as hard. I continued to work but I didn't put extra effort in.' (upper ability)*

*'When I got my first certificate I felt proud because I could show my mum I'd been working well. I got really excited and put it in a frame. I didn't get another certificate that year and I felt really disappointed. I gave up for that year and tried again the next year.'* (middle ability)

*'You don't really need certificates to show that you've done well because you know when you've done well.'* (upper ability)

*'I know when I've done something well because the teacher's comments tell me and the way she marks my work.'* (middle ability)

*'My certificates are on my wall and are important to me because over the years I've collected so many of them.'* (statemented child)

# Behaviour management

Many teachers feel, in their hearts, that external rewards are unnecessary, but feel confused by advice they have been given that children's behaviour should be managed by explicit use of external rewards. This might work for certain children, but I have now had a great deal of feedback from teachers who have created individual behaviour target cards, which are used in the same way as writing target cards, with the focus being the meeting of the target rather than a reward. The system works just as well without external rewards as with them and, in most cases, leads to more sustained improvement. Too often, children strive to win the reward then revert to previous bad behaviour.

# Public celebrations

Whether children's achievements should be celebrated publicly or privately is another issue about self-esteem and its impact on progress. When the focus is the **learning**, research shows that standing in front of the class or school is entirely appropriate. Sharing assemblies, if focused on the work (the learning intention, how it was achieved and so on) are an excellent way of modelling excellence for children and teachers. The same is true for asking children to read out words or phrases or sharing work in the class. If the focus is the work rather than the child, the emphasis is on learning rather than personal feelings.

When the achievement is personal to the child and the **child** becomes the focus of the public celebration, research shows that children's progress and self-esteem is often diminished (Ames, 1992). Again, we need to look carefully at what is happening when children stand in front of their peers. Studies have again shown that the same three groups of children get to stand out the front more than other children: special needs, bright and naughty. The invisibility factor is again at play when the public celebration takes place – children appear to be pleased to be picked out and the rest of the class or school duly smiles and applauds. In the controlled environment of the classroom or the assembly, this is not surprising. But how many children are secretly thinking *'It's her again – why not me?'* or *'My work has been interrupted – I've forgotten what I'm doing now'* or *'I could do that two years ago'*? While many children might genuinely feel pleased at other's achievements, if there is even the slightest chance that, outside the safety of the classroom or hall, one unkind child might say something derogatory to a congratulated child, surely we cannot afford to take that chance.

## *About being read out in assembly...*

*'When you try hard and your name doesn't get called out, you feel disappointed so you feel you don't want to try again because the teacher never notices.'* (middle ability)

*'I feel good when I have been noticed.'* (lower ability)

*'I think you should keep it between your class and your teacher.'* (lower ability)

*'I like the Friday assemblies, but it is embarrassing when your name is read out.'* (middle ability)

*'I don't think I should be in the celebration book all the time because I've got to give other people a chance – it can't always be me.'* (top ability)

*'I don't like the whole school knowing I have achieved something. I feel kind of shy.'* (upper ability)

*'I feel, once you go in the celebration book lots of times, people call you goody-goody and they get an idea about you that you always behave good. I don't like that.'* (upper ability)

*'When you get put in the Celebration Book sometimes they put "You have achieved good writing, keep it up". You get embarrassed because the whole school knows you couldn't do it before but now you can.'*

*'Some teachers put your name in the Celebration Book because you haven't been put in before – comments in books are more important.'*

*'Once Ms X asked us whose name hadn't been mentioned in the Celebration Book so she added the names that had been left out.'*

Of course we still need to encourage children to be 'good citizens'. Instead of a chart which lists the different ways children can get a sticker or other external reward, why not head the chart *'You and I will celebrate your achievement if you....'*?

# Praise versus encouragement

The natural impulse of a teacher is to praise children for their efforts. However, the language of praise can have varying effects on children's self-esteem and ability to be self-evaluative and independent. A culture of excess praise can produce a classroom of 'praise junkies'. The following quotations from a 'High Scope' (1995) publication illustrate the complexities of praise:

*'Praise is like other forms of reward which discourage children from judging for themselves what is right and wrong. Praise may lead to dependency because children come to rely on the authority figure to tell them what is right or wrong, good or bad.'*

(Kamii, 1984)

*'Some students are particularly adept at pulling praise from teachers by smiling or beaming proudly, showing off work, and even communicating an expectation of praise. This praise, however, may have a negative effect such as diminishing a child's sense of worth and struggle for independence.'*

(Brophy, 1981)

*'Students frequently try to read or check the teacher's eyes for signs of approval or disapproval. Praise lowered students' confidence in their answers and reduced the number of verbal responses they offered.'*

(Rowe, 1974)

*'Praise can actually lessen self-motivation and cause children to become dependent on rewards. Praise may be useful in motivating students to learn by rote, but it may actually discourage problem-solving.'*

(Martin, 1977)

'High Scope' suggests that encouragement strategies are more appropriate for a learning culture. Specific suggestions include:

- ■ With younger children, participate in their play, following their lead.

- ■ Encourage children to describe their efforts, ideas and products by asking open-ended questions – *"What can you tell me about...", "How did you...", "I notice you've ... what will you do next?"* This gives them the power to become self-evaluative.

- ■ Acknowledge children's work and ideas by making specific comments. Say *"That is the first time I've seen you put that puzzle together, Donnie. You worked on it for a long time."* This is a conversation starter, whereas *"Good work, Lisa!"* can communicate the message that the conversation is ended and the child is dismissed.

This final quotation comes from *Inside the Black Box*, summarising all the researchers' findings about the importance of the teacher's role in raising children's self-esteem:

*Where the classroom culture focuses on rewards, "gold stars", grades or place-in-the-class ranking, then pupils look for the ways to obtain the best marks rather than at the needs of their learning. The reported consequence is that where they have any choice, pupils avoid difficult tasks. They also spend time and energy looking for the "right answer". Many are reluctant to ask questions out of fear of failure. Pupils who encounter difficulties and poor results are led to believe that they lack ability, and this belief leads them to attribute their difficulties to a defect in themselves about which they cannot do a great deal. So they "retire hurt", avoid investing effort in learning which could only lead to disappointment, and try to build up their self-esteem in other ways. Whilst the high achievers can do well in such a culture, the overall result is to enhance the frequency and the extent of underachievement. What is needed is a culture of success, backed by a belief that all can achieve.*

(Black and Wiliam, 1998)

Raising self-esteem is, it seems, something we need to take very seriously. To recap the aspects of formative assessment where this has been explicitly mentioned:

1   Focus on learning by involving children in creating success criteria and looking at what is to be learnt rather than what is to be done.

2   Encourage children to be self-evaluative during plenary sessions and during the course of a lesson.

3   When children find something difficult or are stuck, use language which shows that difficulty enables us to find out what is needed for new learning to take place.

4   Give the message to children that if they have not understood your instructions, it is *your* responsibility.

5   Make all feedback focus on learning rather than effort.

6   Encourage children to self-mark and be involved in paired marking, looking for success and improvement against learning intentions.

7   Organise individual targets with an ipsative focus: build on previous attainment.

8   Remove any labels which allow children to compare grades or levels across the class.

9   Replace external rewards with explicit focus on the achievement gained, celebrating privately, face-to-face rather than publicly.

10  Replace meaningless praise with encouragement.

**INSET ideas**

The best INSET approach is to familiarise all educators in the school with the research findings, explore children's views, give neutral starting points, and wait until formative assessment is firmly established before reviewing the use of rewards.

# 9 Using this book to make a difference

The order of this book provides, in general terms, the suggested order of implementation in the school. Schools involved in formative assessment have found it much more effective to introduce the strategies one at a time, getting them embedded and making sure everyone is empowered, before moving on to the next. I suggest that a year is spent introducing formative assessment in the first instance, with the second year reviewing the strategies and making decisions about wider issues.

| Timing | Strategy |
| --- | --- |
| Half-term to a term, depending on current situation | Review current planning to ensure clarity of learning intentions. Every teacher should be able to see the learning intention of each lesson on his or her short-term plan. Pre-print learning intentions in schemes of work or medium-term plans. |
| Half-term | Introduce and trial sharing learning intentions. Feedback and continue. |
| Half-term | Introduce and trial pupil self-evaluation. Feedback and continue. |
| Half-term to a term | Introduce and trial oral and written (coded) feedback against learning intentions. Feedback and continue. |
| | Feedback all the strategies so far, to see how more time has changed their impact and teacher's expertise. |
| Term | Introduce writing target cards or flaps. Feedback and continue. |
| Half-term | Discuss self-esteem in the light of the formative assessment strategies and review current practice. |

# Effecting change

One of the most daunting aspects of having responsibility in a school is in finding the best ways of effecting change and introducing new initiatives. On my courses, I have asked participants to brainstorm all the things that *can* go wrong. From that the following table has been developed: the problem is stated, the reason for the problem discussed and the best strategies for dealing with the problem shared. The list could be much longer, but the strategies here can be applied to many situations where change produces difficulty.

# Managing staff

| Problem | Reason | Strategies |
|---|---|---|
| Teachers always seeing negative aspects | They want an easy life. They don't feel valued. They feel threatened. Enjoy being the Devil's Advocate. People don't like change and new things – we have to get them through those feelings. | Be positive. Don't react in a defensive, negative way. Try to raise self-esteem. Work with the people who are interested in initiatives and use them for a pilot to be fed back to the rest. Approach the most negative people before the meeting and ask for their advice – take them into your confidence about possible difficulties with staff etc. – they often respond to being involved and made to feel important by being more positive than anyone! Before running a staff meeting on any new initiative, go to every member of staff over a period of time, discussing it with them personally and asking for their views and advice. By the meeting it is usually a 'fait accompli' or, at least, they are on your side and discussions are conducted professionally. |

| Problem | Reason | Strategies |
|---------|--------|------------|
| 'I've seen it all before' | They've taught for 25 years the same way. Things do come round and can be depressing. | Need more contact with other schools and teachers. **See above** |
| 'Tell me what to do' | They don't understand the new initiative. Feel pressurised. Don't want the burden of extra work – too busy. | Give support. Whole school needs to look at areas in more depth. Staff have to be involved in the process. Have more small group discussions so they have to think for themselves. |
| Negative body language | Not interested. Don't like the person leading the staff meeting. Tired at the end of the day. | Involve the staff in the meeting. Make it active and short. If necessary, head should confront the person privately and say it is noticeable and is unprofessional and must stop (asking if the person needs support first, etc.). |
| People not being able to say what they think | Dominant personalities, hierarchy. | Carefully select small groups in meetings (e.g. group people by equal status rather than mixed, so all will feel confident to speak). |
| Dominant personalities | Feel they have high status. Appear secure. Trying to prove they are 'good' teachers. | See above + management of meeting. |
| Falls asleep | Tired, old, pregnant, ill, been out all night, bored. | Vary styles of meeting. Keep windows open, strong black coffee, chocolate for energy. Ground rules needed. |
| Viewing new initiatives as more work | Overloaded, asked to do too much. | Trialling periods to know the worth of the initiative. Prioritising. Provide release to support new initiatives. Arrange feedback meetings about something specific. |

| Problem | Reason | Strategies |
|---|---|---|
| No definite decisions are made or are obvious | Poor management. Meeting rambles so needs more time. | Agenda must itemise. Chair must make statement of what stage has been reached for each item, even if this is that the thing will have to be carried over or become a working party or small group discussion. Sometimes decisions can't be made because there needs to be some action to see if it works rather than keep talking hypothetically. Trial and review everything. |
| They agree but carry on regardless | Know they can. Want a quiet life at meeting but know they can get away with it. | Monitoring issue and feedback meetings needed where everyone must contribute. Reminders sent a few days before. |
| Staff not airing views at meeting but outside | Intimidated – large groups. Unsure of themselves, inadequate, lack of trust. Not feeling views will be valued, based on past experience. Not fully aware – not taking on board their roles and responsibilities. | Small groups in meetings. Long-term aim to change ethos. Recognise the problem and identify causes (personalities, history). Set out clear role definitions and job descriptions. |
| Not enough follow-up meetings to ensure change occurs | Poor planning – expecting to achieve too much. | Year group or Key Stage meetings to feed into main meeting. In advance ask for people's written views by a certain date, although it is better to talk to them. Better planning by management of the year's meetings |

| Problem | Reason | Strategies |
|---|---|---|
| Decisions are made but they are impossible to carry out | Panic – too much change needed, not knowing where to start. Lack of organisation/resources. Not delegating, monitoring roles within tasks. | Break down into manageable chunks via an action plan. Team needed with clear allocation of responsibility. Feedback to staff – feasibility, manageability. Keep people informed. Feed back to staff on positive achievement. |
| People who don't ask for help | Lack of confidence, fear of seeming a failure, older staff expect that they should know, NQTs fear of being judged. Demoralisation. Don't know who to ask – think they are too busy. | We need to ask questions. Monitoring. Structured programme of observation and positive feedback. Clear role and responsibility structure. Senior management check hierarchy of monitoring is working. Mentor in year group for new staff. |

# Keeping it all going

Once the formative assessment strategies have been introduced, it is important to keep momentum in the following ways:

■ Make sure the strategies are monitored, especially by classroom observation (see Chapter 7).

■ Make the strategies visually obvious throughout the school.

■ Refer to the strategies during whole-school events such as assemblies, so that all staff and pupils know the common language of achievement.

■ Write an assessment policy, which outlines exactly how formative assessment is carried out, under the headings of the various chapters. Make sure everyone has copies of this.

- Produce parent-friendly news-sheets along the way, as each strategy is introduced, so that parents are fully informed and encouraged to support their children's new development.

- Produce summaries of the assessment policy when it is finished, to show all relevant parties.

- During OFSTED inspections, make sure the Registered Inspector is fully informed about all the formative assessment strategies in the school, and their rationale.

- Continue to review the strategies in action, consulting all parties involved – especially children.

# Meeting OFSTED demands

The current framework for inspection makes clear the emphasis on teaching and learning and formative assessment (see page 5). However, the legacy of the pre-Dearing days still haunts many schools, with teachers often involved in unnecessary assessment procedures because they do not want to risk change. Schools who have had successful OFSTED inspections always have one thing in common: they are confident about their practice. What matters is that every teacher is clear about the rationale for the practices in the school – *why* you are doing what you do.

When teachers are questioned, everyone should give the same response, indicating coherence and consistency. If OFSTED inspectors ask questions like *'Why don't you have…..?'*, respond by answering the underlying question: the original OFSTED criterion. There are a number of ways the OFSTED criteria can be satisfied, so you should not be expected to follow any set procedures, only to fulfil the criteria. If their questions are about the method of fulfilling the criteria, show how you are in fact meeting the criteria, but by a different method. For instance, an inspector might only have seen certain methods of tracking children's progress and expect to see that way in your school. Explaining the ways in which your school tracks children's progress to meet the OFSTED criteria shows confidence and well-thought-out policies. As tracking children's progress is a common concern, typical strategies are shown below:

# Tracking children's progress

## Summative measures

- End-of-year levels for each child tracked against targets set for Year 6;
- any other school or class tests.

## Formative measures

- Following schemes of work which are aligned to levels;
- using assessment information to inform planning (assessment jottings, messy short-term plans);
- taking account of self-evaluation comments;
- marking against learning intentions;
- individual writing targets;
- any other individual targets (i.e. IEPs);
- looking through children's work in the context of lessons.

### RECORD KEEPING

| Teachers' records | Children's work |
|---|---|
| Assessment notes on weekly planning documents. | Written feedback on children's work. |
| Summative record booklet. | |
| • End of year level for core subjects and ICT- all years.<br>• NFER non verbal reasoning-all years<br>• Reading ages- Y3, Y4, Y5<br>• TA and SATS results Y6<br>• QCA results Y3, Y4 and Y5 | Individual target cards for<br><br>• Number<br>• writing |
| HT to keep records above plus teachers' annual forecasts on Assessment Manager as an aid to Target Setting. | |
| End of year report to parents | |
| Internal transfer grid. | |
| Statutory transfer sheet to receiving schools. | |
| Exemplary School Portfolio for Core subjects and eventually ICT. | |

*Fig. 9.1 Extract from one school's assessment policy*

By following the strategies outlined in this book, you will be getting to the heart of OFSTED's requirements – ensuring that teaching and learning is the central focus of the school. The following extract from an inspection report (Fig. 9.2) shows how OFSTED responded to a school where formative assessment strategies are well established.

---

## HOW WELL ARE PUPILS TAUGHT?

15. The overall quality of teaching is good and this effectively enables pupils to learn and make progress. Teaching has improved since the last inspection and reflects the good attention paid by the school to improving standards. Effective implementation of the National Literacy and Numeracy Strategies together with improved systems of planning guide teachers well. They lead to well-organised lessons with good attention to pupils' learning. Good attention is paid, for example, to the provision of resources in many lessons. This enables lessons to proceed at a good pace with little lost time. Many teachers set effective time targets that add additional impetus to lessons and encourage pupils to work hard. Homework is used effectively by teachers. A good range of activities is set, many of which play important roles in promoting pupils' learning. For example, pupils make notes of the styles of news reporting and are therefore able to contribute well to a discussion of these. This leads to effective writing when using these styles. Some extended pieces of work are set and these enable pupils to research and display their work in a variety of forms.

16. Very good relationships are established throughout the school and teachers use these effectively to promote a good atmosphere for learning. Teachers have good questioning skills and use them well. Pupils are effectively challenged and questioning ensures that they think carefully about their work. **Teachers praise pupils' responses appropriately and give recognition and respect to their ideas and opinions**. Pupils respond well to this and develop confidence, allowing them to give answers willingly. The high quality of relationships allows teachers to have good control of classes. Lessons are conducted with a calm and considerate approach that encourages pupils to do well.

17. **Teachers' planning pays good attention to the clear identification of what pupils need to learn. This is invariably discussed with pupils at the beginning of lessons. As a result, pupils are given secure purpose to their activities and this steers lessons well. Both teachers and pupils are able to assess informally how well the lesson has gone.** Introductions and explanations are generally appropriately paced and set out the activities well. In a small minority of lessons, however, teachers spend too long in introductory sessions. This leads to some losses of pupils' attention and impatience to begin

that detract from their progress. When teachers have a number of groups working, they often focus effectively on one group. However, this leaves other groups with less supervision and in some lessons their pace of work slows.

18. **Most lessons include useful discussion periods at the end that allow pupils to reflect on their learning. Teachers often use these for informal assessment of pupils' successes. Detailed assessment systems are developing with very effective systems in place in English. These are being extended to mathematics and other subjects. The identification of pupils' individual targets in English is good and often promotes learning well. Teachers effectively use the good systems for ensuring that pupils keep these in mind as they undertake their work.** This helps pupils to make good progress as they reflect on what they need to do to improve their work.

39. **The school has effective strategies for assessing and monitoring pupils' academic performance.** Teachers maintain **records of learning that are effectively passed on** from the infant school. They give teachers a picture of pupils' progress and attainment in English, mathematics, science and information technology year by year. They are usefully related to National Curriculum levels of attainment. **The rigorous and very effective assessment procedures in English have been extended successfully to mathematics. Through their marking, teachers set clear specific targets for individual pupils that are periodically reviewed and modified in light of their progress. This system is well established in English and is clearly leading to higher standards.** It is still developing but beginning to show some positive trends in mathematics. There are plans to extend the scheme further into other subjects. Teachers make good use of a range of standard and optional tests to monitor pupils' progress and to set overall targets. They use their assessments less effectively when planning work for pupils of different levels of attainment. As a result, not all pupils are consistently making all the progress they are capable of across the curriculum.

40. **Pupils are increasingly involved in setting their own targets and in reflecting thoughtfully on what they have learned in lessons. This gives them a clear understanding of their own success, progress and what they need to do to improve.** For example one pupil in Year 4 had been involved in agreeing a target to put full stops and capital letters in her future writing. **She was reminded of this objective before each new piece of work by a card attached to her book. Teachers draw pupils' attention to displayed questions that help them to evaluate their own learning in subjects across the curriculum. These include prompts such as "What did you find difficult?" and "What helped you?"**

*Fig. 9.2 OFSTED inspection report extract (my emphases)*

# Conclusion

*Targeting Assessment in the Primary Classroom* set the scene for this book, outlining the beginnings of formative assessment strategies. *Unlocking Formative Assessment* illustrates the enormous leaps being made by teachers in primary schools all over the country in developing these strategies. The feedback from teachers applying the strategies has been overwhelming. As the research demonstrates, formative assessment makes a significant difference to children's progress – in their ability to be confident, critical learners, to achieve more than ever before and in raising their self-esteem. In a world of continuing pressure, it is good to know that we are making a real difference to children's lives.

# References

Abbott, J. (1999) 'Battery hens or free range chickens: what kind of education for what kind of world?', *Journal of the 21st Century Learning Initiative*, January pp1–12.

Ames, C. and Ames, R. (1984) 'Systems of student and teacher motivation: toward a qualitative definition', *Journal of Educational Psychology*, 76, 535–56.

Ames, C. (1992) 'Classrooms: goals, structures and student motivation', *Journal of Educational Psychology*, 84, 261–71.

Assessment Reform Group (1999) *Assessment for Learning: Beyond the Black Box*, University of Cambridge School of Education.

Black, P. and Wiliam, D. (1998) 'Assessment and classroom learning', *Assessment in Education*, 5, 1.

Black, P. and Wiliam, D. (1998) *Inside the Black Box: Raising Standards through Classroom Assessment*, London: King's College School of Education.

Brophy, J. E. (1981). 'Teacher praise: a functional analysis', *Review of Educational Research, 51,* 1, p.27 (in High Scope, 1995).

Butler, R. (1988) 'Enhancing and undermining intrinsic motivation; the effects of task-involving and ego-involving evaluation on interest and performance', *British Journal of Educational Psychology*, 58, 1–14.

Clarke, S. (1998) *Targeting Assessment in the Primary Classroom*, Hodder and Stoughton.

Crooks, T. J. (1998) 'The impact of classroom evaluation practices on students', *Review of Educational Research*, 58, 438–81.

Dweck, C. (1986) 'Motivational processes affecting learning', *American Psychologist, 41*, 1041–8.

Elstgeest, J. (1985) 'The right question at the right time', in Harlen, W. (ed.) *Taking the Plunge: how to teach science more effectively*, Heinemann.

Elstgeest, J. (1992) 'Questions and questioning', *Primary Science Review 23*.

Gardner, H., (1993) *Frames of Mind: The Theory of Multiple Intelligences*, Fontana.

Goleman, D. (1996) *Emotional Intelligence: why it can matter more than IQ*, Bloomsbury.

High Scope Educational Research Foundation (1995) *Adult-Child Interaction Participant Guide.*

Hillocks, G. Jr. (1986*). Research on written composition, new directions for teaching*. Urbana, Illinois: National Conference on Research in English.

Kamii, C. (1984). 'Viewpoint: obedience is not enough', *Young Children*, *39*, 4, 13 (in High Scope, 1995).

Knight, S. (2000) *Questions: Assessing and Developing Children's Understanding and Thinking in Literacy*, Manchester School Improvement Service (tel. 0161 610 3333).

Lepper, M. R. and Hodell, M. (1989) 'Intrinsic motivation in the classroom', in C. Ames and R. Ames (eds) *Research on Motivation in the Classroom*, Vol.3, pp. 73–105, San Diego: Academic Press.

Martin, D. L. (1977) 'Your praise can smother learning', *Learning*, *5*, 6, p.51 (in High Scope, 1995).

National Literacy Strategy (1998) Talking in Class, National Centre for Literacy and Numeracy, London House, 59–65 London Street, Reading RG1 4EW.

National Numeracy Project (no date) *Mathematical Vocabulary*, National Centre for Literacy and Numeracy, London House, 59–65 London Street, Reading RG1 4EW.

Nottinghamshire Advisory and Inspection Services, Nottingham County Council (1999) *Target setting with pupils: using small steps in the National Curriculum* (tel. 01623 466700).

OFSTED (1999) *Inspecting mathematics, including Numeracy, in primary and special schools*, Office for Standards in Education.

OFSTED (2000) *Handbook for Inspecting Primary and Nursery schools*, Office for Standards in Education.

QCA (1999*) Keeping Track*, Qualifications & Curriculum Authority.

QCA (1999) *Target Setting and Assessment in the National Literacy Strategy*, Qualifications & Curriculum Authority.

Rowe, M. B. (1974) 'Relation of wait-time and rewards to the development of language, logic and fate control', *Journal of Research in Science Teaching*, *11*, 4, p.292 (in High Scope, 1995).

Sadler, R. (1989) Formative assessment and the design of instructional systems, *Instructional Science*, *18*, 119–44.

Vispoel, W. P. and Austin, J. R. (1995) Success and failure in junior high school: a critical incident approach to understanding students' attributional beliefs, *American Educational Research Journal*, *32*, 2, 377–412.

# Photocopiable resources

## Child-speak writing targets: Levels 1c–4

## INSET handouts

# Child-speak writing targets: Levels 1c–4

## Level 1c: I am learning to:

- write my letters carefully, so other people can recognise them
- get my letters the right way round
- make my letters the right size
- write letters and words that will tell someone else what I mean
- read my writing to other people using the words and letters I have written
- write stories, lists and letters

## Level 1b: I am learning to:

- write in short sentences or groups of words
- write so other people can read my writing without my help
- use a full stop at the end of some sentences
- write stories, lists and letters
- get my letters the right way round most of the time
- write my letters starting in the right place every time

## Level 1a: I am learning to:

- write in short sentences
- use interesting words in my writing
- spell some words right
- write my letters properly all the time
- use a capital letter at the start of a sentence
- use a full stop at the end of a sentence
- write stories, lists and letters

---

# Child-speak writing targets: Levels 1c–4 cont.

## Level 2c: I am learning to:

■ write more and use two or three different ideas

■ link ideas by using words like 'and' and 'then'

■ write a story with a beginning, a middle and an end

■ put a capital letter and a full stop in some of my sentences

■ spell some easy words (such as: back, came, down, from, have, one, school, sister, two, were)

■ use letter sounds to help me write more difficult words

■ think about other words I can spell that sound like the word I want to spell

■ write neatly sitting my letters on the line

## Level 2b: I am learning to:

■ write stories that make sense all the way through

■ write a story in which there is more than one person or animal

■ write a story in which several things happen

■ use interesting and different words in my writing

■ use 'but', 'then' and other words to join sentences

■ use capital letters and full stops for most of my sentences

■ spell correctly on my own easy words that I use a lot

■ use letter patterns to help me spell words (patterns like oo, ck and nt)

■ use rhymes to help me spell words (call, fall, ball, tall)

■ make sure g p j q y all sit on the line

■ make sure t l k f d b are all taller than the other letters

■ make sure I don't put capital letters in the middle of words

**Unlocking Formative Assessment**, by Shirley Clarke, is published by Hodder & Stoughton Educational. The publishers grant permission for photocopies of this sheet to be made for use solely in the purchasing institution.

# Child-speak writing targets: Levels 1c–4 *cont.*

## Level 2a: I am learning to:

- use capital letters and full stops most of the time
- join sentences in different ways (e.g. He kicked the ball against the wall whilst he was waiting for Susie)
- start sentences in different ways (e.g. Although he was tired, he carried on running./Before he could move, the dog ran off.)
- use interesting describing words (adjectives), such as 'an enormous, red lorry' or 'a black stormy night'
- spell many words correctly
- use some 'story language', such as 'One hot summer day...' or 'Many years ago there lived...'
- write a story for other people (e.g. for Year 1 children)
- write information using a title and sub-headings
- write a letter setting it out like a letter should be
- write clearly and neatly all the time

## Level 3c: I am learning to:

- write stories, reports and instructions
- write stories, reports and instructions with clear beginnings, middles and endings
- make sure that the bits of my story or report follow one another in a sensible order
- use words which are suitable for the 'setting' of my story (e.g. a dark, gloomy cave, a golden beach of sand, 'Yo ho ho', said the pirate chief)
- use words to connect my ideas, such as 'when', 'so', 'because', 'although'
- spell many words correctly which have more than one syllable
- write stories with some interesting events happening in the middle
- write interesting endings for my stories

**Unlocking Formative Assessment**, by Shirley Clarke, is published by Hodder & Stoughton Educational. The publishers grant permission for photocopies of this sheet to be made for use solely in the purchasing institution.

# Child-speak writing targets: Levels 1c–4 *cont.*

## Level 3b: I am learning to:

- begin to describe people and things with some details (e.g. She was a tall, thin lady with a blue hat)
- start to describe people's feelings and thoughts
- include some conversation in my stories and begin to use speech marks
- use question marks and exclamation marks
- begin to use alliteration (e.g. William wears white wellies)
- join my letters
- make a short list of the important things in a story which I have read
- describe where my story happens so the reader can imagine what it is like

## Level 3a: I am learning to:

- read through my work to check for mistakes (proof read)
- change parts of my work to improve it (re-draft)
- describe why someone does something and say how they feel using appropriate words
- use humour or suspense in my story
- write in a number of ways – stories, lists, poems, reports, letters
- use the correct way of setting out my writing (e.g. set out a letter correctly)
- begin to use more interesting ways of joining sentences (e.g. She began to put the balls in the box, starting with the big ones.)

# Child-speak writing targets: Levels 1c–4 *cont.*

## Level 4: I am learning to:

■ make sure everything is in the right order in my stories and there are no gaps

■ pace my stories well

■ show significant interaction between characters, saying how they feel and react

■ show what kind of people my characters are by what they say and do

■ be aware of the reader of my story, by making comments to them

■ use paragraphs to separate new subjects or events

■ use commas where there is more than one phrase or in a list

■ always use speech marks, question marks and exclamation marks appropriately

■ use well-chosen vocabulary, including connectives for order and emphasis

■ begin to use adverbs (e.g. He whistles a tune happily)

**Unlocking Formative Assessment**, by Shirley Clarke, is published by Hodder & Stoughton Educational. The publishers grant permission for photocopies of this sheet to be made for use solely in the purchasing institution.

# Unlocking Formative Assessment: *INSET handout*

## The characteristics of assessment that promote learning:

■ it is embedded in a view of teaching and learning of which it is an essential part;

■ it involves sharing learning goals with pupils;

■ it aims to help pupils to know and to recognise the standards they are aiming for;

■ it involves pupils in self-assessment;

■ it provides feedback which leads to pupils recognising their next steps and how to take them;

■ it is underpinned by confidence that every student can improve;

■ it involves both teachers and pupils reviewing and reflecting on assessment data.
*(Assessment for Learning: Beyond the Black Box,* Assessment Reform Group, 1999)

## Inhibiting factors:

■ a tendency for teachers to assess quantity of work and presentation rather than quality of learning;

■ greater attention given to marking and grading, much of it tending to lower the self-esteem of pupils, rather than to providing advice for improvement;

■ a strong emphasis on comparing pupils with each other which demoralises the less successful learners;

■ teachers' feedback to pupils often serves social and managerial purposes rather than helping them to learn more effectively;

■ teachers not knowing enough about their pupils' learning needs.
*(Assessment for Learning: Beyond the Black Box,* Assessment Reform Group, 1999)

# Unlocking Formative Assessment: *INSET handout*

## Key features of effective planning

### At the long-term stage

- Learning intentions are unambiguous and clear, establishing whether knowledge, skill or concept and providing, e.g. statements to clarify and ensure consistency of interpretation

- Learning intentions are seen as a menu rather than a list to be tackled in order

- Learning intentions cannot have equal weighting

- Bring together the best of pre-NC planning with the best of today's: rigorous learning intentions underpinned by meaningful learning contexts rather than a delivery model

- Aim for as few activities as possible linked with grouped learning intentions, rather than a one-to-one correspondence

- In using long-term plans, consider how well children are performing against the learning intentions first, then, in the light of that, reconsider the planned activities for relevance (OFSTED: 'Use assessment information to inform planning')

### At the short-term stage

- Learning intentions need to be next to or clearly linked to each activity rather than in a bank, in order to be the first point of reference in planning and beginning the lesson

- Short-term plans should be messy by the end of the week, with changes made wherever the teacher changes her mind about how planned lessons might need to be altered. Assessment notes made on the plan should inform future planning only (see statutory requirements) rather than attempt to track individual progress. Evaluations of lessons are unnecessary on a day-to-day basis

# Unlocking Formative Assessment: *INSET handout*

## Key features of sharing learning intentions

- Make it an expectation
- Separate the learning intention from the activity instructions
- State the learning intention ('We are learning to . . .), then activity, then together create success criteria
- Ask 'How will we know we've achieved this?' in order to involve them in creating success criteria, if they can
- Ask children to repeat it, or read it back to you
- The power of the visual image – get learning intention and success criteria displayed – perhaps 'We are learning to' and 'We'll know we've achieved it because . . .' or 'So we need to . . .' or similar.
- *Fluent* writers write the learning intention as the title

---

**Learning intention in teacher's plan:** To explore narrative order and identify and map out the main stages of a story.

**Shared with children:**

**Learning intention:** *We are learning to order our own and other stories.*

**Success criteria:** *We will have ordered the story we looked at into our own story plan.*

**ASIDE (oral only):** *Ordering is an important skill in reading, writing and maths.*

---

**Learning intention in teacher's plan:** To be able to use and apply doubling and halving.

**Shared with children:**

**Learning intention:** *We are learning to use doubling and halving in everyday life.*

**Success criteria:** *We can show more than one way to double and halve numbers.*

**ASIDE (oral only):** *This will help you in everyday life, when shopping for two of the same thing, etc. . . .*

---

**Learning intention in teacher's plan:** To recognise numbers to 10.

**Shared with children:**

**Learning intention:** *We are learning to say or recognise the numbers we write down.*

**Success criteria:** *We can tell someone the names of all these numbers.*

**ASIDE (oral only):** *You'll need to know numbers on buses and doors, etc. . . .*

---

# Unlocking Formative Assessment: *INSET handout*

## Key features of self-evaluation

■ The emphasis is on thinking and articulating, not writing

■ Questions are easier to answer:
  – after a short period of time
  – if related to the learning intention
  – if visually displayed
  – if modelled first by the teacher

■ Articulation can be by brainstorm, in small groups or pairs

■ It cannot be systematic in accounting for each child's responses: it establishes a constant feature of lessons

■ A range of questions displayed as a poster, as a menu for the ends of lessons, broadens the scope for analysis and raising self-esteem:

---

### Self evaluation:
#### thinking about what happens when we are learning

*(Choose one and add the words of the learning intention)*

- **What really made you think while you were learning to ... ?**

- **What helped you** (e.g. a friend, the teacher, new equipment, a book, your own thinking) **when something got tricky about learning to ... ?**

- **What do you need more help with about learning to ... ?**

- **What are you most pleased with about learning to ... ?**

- **What have you learnt that is new about ... (quote learning intention)?**

- **How would you change this activity for another group/class who were learning to ... ?**

---

**Unlocking Formative Assessment**, by Shirley Clarke, is published by Hodder & Stoughton Educational. The publishers grant permission for photocopies of this sheet to be made for use solely in the purchasing institution.

# Unlocking Formative Assessment: *INSET handout*

## Key features of effective feedback

■ Effective feedback consists of information about the learning intention of the task, pointing out success and improvement needs against the learning intention

■ Limit the task demands and subsequent feedback: give feedback only about what children were asked to pay attention to – do not give feedback on what they were not

■ Ask children to focus on one factor at a time rather than all at once

■ Focus on spelling in other contexts releasing children from spelling as a constant criterion – children spell correctly when they know how to spell the word, not when they don't

■ For distance marking:
  - make sure they can read it
  - make sure they can understand it
  - give set lesson time for children to read it (3 minutes)
  - give set lesson time for one focused improvement to be made (5 minutes)

■ Use coded marking against the learning intention for accessibility and manageability

■ Use a 'closing the gap' prompt to structure improvement points:
either – a reminder prompt
        – a scaffolded prompt
        – an example prompt

■ Avoid external rewards, which act as a grade, demotivating the less able

■ Inform parents of the school's feedback policy

**Unlocking Formative Assessment**, by Shirley Clarke, is published by Hodder & Stoughton Educational. The publishers grant permission for photocopies of this sheet to be made for use solely in the purchasing institution.

# Unlocking Formative Assessment: *INSET handout*

## Key features of effective individual target setting

■ At Reception, children have informal targets, usually based on social skills or early writing stages

■ Children from Year 1 have copies of all the targets for the level or sub-level above the level they have achieved, written in child speak if inaccessible – they can then look ahead and determine next focus

■ Target lists should NOT have number of level (e.g. 2a) visible, to ensure children are fully motivated and task related, avoiding comparison of levels and possible demoralisation or demotivation

■ Child and teacher decide on one target at a time

■ The current target needs to be visible while the children are working (flap or card) to keep it in child's and teacher's mind

■ Children and teacher need to have a symbol (e.g. T) which is written on current work to indicate when they think a target has been met – this creates a buffer for teacher to decide when to speak to the child about the target

■ Targets should be achievable and quantified clearly – lasting approximately 4–6 weeks

**Unlocking Formative Assessment**, by Shirley Clarke, is published by Hodder & Stoughton Educational. The publishers grant permission for photocopies of this sheet to be made for use solely in the purchasing institution.